T0197028

# MOTHERHOOD COMES NATURALLY

*(and other vicious lies)*

# MOTHERHOOD COMES NATURALLY

*(and other vicious lies)*

# JILL SMOKLER

**G**

GALLERY BOOKS

NEW YORK    LONDON    TORONTO    SYDNEY    NEW DELHI

# G

Gallery Books
A Division of Simon & Schuster, Inc.
1230 Avenue of the Americas
New York, NY 10020

Copyright © 2013 by Jill Smokler

First Gallery Books hardcover edition April 2013

GALLERY BOOKS and colophon are registered trademarks of Simon & Schuster, Inc.

For information about special discounts for bulk purchases, please contact Simon & Schuster Special Sales at 1-866-506-1949 or *business@simonandschuster.com.*

The Simon & Schuster Speakers Bureau can bring authors to your live event. For more information or to book an event contact the Simon & Schuster Speakers Bureau at 1-866-248-3049 or visit our website at *www.simonspeakers.com.*

Logo designed by Jill Smokler
Illustrations by Amy Saidens

Manufactured in the United States of America

10   9   8   7   6   5   4   3   2   1

Library of Congress Cataloging-in-Publication Data is on file.

ISBN 978-1-5011-6204-6
ISBN 978-1-4767-2838-4(ebook)

*For my amazing children,*
*who gave me a voice,*
*and for my husband,*
*who makes me a better everything.*

# CONTENTS

## MOTHERHOOD IS . . .

Motherhood is middle-of-the-night wake-up calls for a glass of water or a fan or a night-light or a blanket or a bear or a kiss or a Band-Aid.

Motherhood is making lunch after lunch after lunch after lunch only to find the healthy contents stuffed behind a car seat.

Motherhood is all of your spending money.

Motherhood is not remembering what it's like to get a full night's sleep.

Motherhood is wiping more shit than you ever thought you'd see in your entire life.

Motherhood is a car so filthy that you are embarrassed to let your own husband see it.

Motherhood is hearing the word *why* at least a hundred times a day and, most of the time, not having an answer.

Motherhood is knowing, just from the touch of a forehead, almost exactly what your child's temperature is.

Motherhood is finally appreciating your own mother.

Motherhood is fantasizing over reaching the bottom of the laundry pile, knowing full well that it's never going to happen, and even if it does, someone will end up puking or peeing themselves three seconds later.

Motherhood is singing all the words to your kids' favorite songs even though they annoy the hell out of you.

Motherhood is never feeling at peace unless all of your children are with you, under your own roof.

Motherhood is always feeling mildly sick but never being able to wallow in your own misery.

Motherhood is never peeing or showering in peace.

Motherhood is using your sleeves to wipe runny noses and your spit to clean dirty faces.

Motherhood is not even wanting to say "I told you so" even though you *did* tell them so, countless times.

Motherhood is when, just as you want to curl up into a ball of pure exhaustion and desperation, one of your children suddenly farts or burps or does something spontaneously funny and you forget how exhausted you just were.

Motherhood is the moment you pause and look at your children, all piled on your bed, breathless and rosy-cheeked, and think that the only things that really matter in the world are right there in front of you. They are yours, and they are worth every sacrifice and sleepless night.

And then, it's the moment, two seconds later, when one of them will accidentally kick the other one on the arm and the other will bite into the offending calf in retaliation and you will wish, for the hundredth time that day, that you could just press the rewind button to savor the peace and joy of your perfect, serene children for more than an instant.

Rinse and repeat. A million times.

That's motherhood.

## INTRODUCTION

What were you told about motherhood before you had children? That you wouldn't believe how much you love your kids? That your heart would break when they hurt? That you would do anything for them? All true, without a doubt.

But there are some other things you might have been told, too: That parenting strengthens a marriage. That it gets easier after those exhausting days of having a newborn. That being at home with young kids is fulfilling. Are those always true? No. Not for me, at least. On the pages of this book, you'll find everything I thought to be true about parenting . . . before I actually was one.

Some of the lies in this collection may be totally relatable to you, while others might make you question my morals. That's okay, because Scary Mommy has always been about lifting the veil on motherhood and helping women find comfort—and humor—in other mothers' experiences.

What some of us consider a burden, others view as a blessing. And what some of us are willing to do with a smile on our face, others would prefer a lobotomy to. Volunteering in a kindergarten classroom; taking the kids trick-or-treating for hours on Halloween; reading bedtime story after bedtime story when we should be sleeping ourselves. Some of us love those particular moments and some of us wish them away, in exchange for whatever moments we savor most. It's one of the many beauties of motherhood: like DNA, no woman's experience is the same as anyone else's.

I would never claim to be an expert on parenting—far from it. This is not a parenting manual or a how-to guide; rather, think of it as a coping resource; a place to turn when you feel like the only mother on earth who isn't handling the gig with utter grace and ease. It's a way to find some humor in the not so easy parts of motherhood. Because as wonderful as motherhood is, it's also the hardest job in the world, and we'd all go crazy if we couldn't laugh at ourselves.

*That's* one thing I know to be true.

*Lie #1*

# MOTHERHOOD COMES NATURALLY

I am the CEO of a Fortune 500 company. I speak three languages. I have negotiated multimillion-dollar deals without breaking a sweat. However, just thinking about bedtime for my three kids makes me want to vomit.

*—Scary Mommy Confession #208830*

Once upon a time, I found myself unexpectedly expecting and scared out of my mind. If I clearly wasn't responsible enough to practice safe sex, it was pretty safe to say that I wasn't responsible enough to bring a child into the world. A few days after I peed on every kind of stick the drugstore had to offer, I found myself at the gynecologist for further confirmation. As I hyperventilated on the table, flashing back to that night of one too many margaritas, I was consoled by a kind nurse. She was a sweet older woman in faded Dora the Explorer scrubs, with years of experience and wisdom under her belt. "Honey," she confidently told me in her soothing James Earl Jonesey voice, "motherhood is the most natural thing in the world. You'll love it."

That was the first time I ever listened to a grown woman in cartoon-themed hospital scrubs, and the last. She wasn't *all* wrong; the latter part of her wisdom has certainly proven to be true. Almost ten years have passed since that day, and I love being a mother like I have never loved anything before in my life. I have three beautiful and hilarious and amazing children whom I would lay down my life for without thinking twice. It is, without a doubt, the best thing that has ever happened to me. But, natural? No, I'm afraid not. Motherhood doesn't always come all that naturally.

Things that come naturally to me: Food. Sleep. Comfort. Privacy. Basically, all of the things that pregnancy and children have cruelly robbed from me.

Let's start with pregnancy—not exactly what I would call natural. I spent almost all of my nine months puking my guts out. For the first time in my life, I couldn't eat what *I* wanted to eat, since I was being held hostage by this mystery creature who dictated my diet. I craved tuna sandwiches on white bread layered with potato chips, and my normal staple breakfast of Cheerios suddenly made me queasy. The baby I didn't know prevented me from finding a comfortable position to sleep in and ensured that I ran to the bathroom every three seconds to pee. I had a hard enough time getting used to sharing a bathroom with my husband when we first moved in together. My body—the only thing that was ever mine and all mine—now belonged to someone else. What's natural about that?

Labor was another extraordinarily unnatural event for me. Sitting in a chair, legs practically over my head, I felt like some sort of freak show contortionist on display for the doctors and nurses. I half expected someone to start making popcorn. I spent much of my time in labor envying those women who sit on a toilet and shit out a baby. Bizarre, sure, but at least they're alone, in a room where they're used to expelling things, having gravity work for them rather than against them. That sounds a hell of a lot more natural to me.

Once the baby comes, you're suddenly supposed to know exactly what is best for the child, as if mother's intuition arrives along with the onset of breast milk. Guess what? It doesn't. That first car ride home together felt as natural as me driving a spaceship straight to Mars.

The first few days and weeks home with a baby, I felt more like I was hired to play the role of Mother than actually *be* a mother. Wasn't I supposed to have changed overnight, suddenly in possession of all the answers? That's what I expected, at least, but I remained the same exact person I was before, except now I was responsible for a human being other than myself. I remember a friend telling me that cries were just the baby's way of communicating and I could decode them if I tried hard enough. Was she hungry? Hot? Cold? Wet? Clearly, I didn't speak baby because every scream sounded exactly the same to me: like a baby crying.

And it didn't become more natural with baby number two even if I fooled myself into thinking that I had the hang of things. I didn't. When Ben was a few months old, he got sick. Not *really* sick—just a lingering cough, thanks to a minor cold.

I'd been through this sort of winter before with Lily, so I knew the drill. Hell, I was an expert by now! He was stuffy but smiley, and I knew in my heart that he was just fine. There was no sinking feeling in my gut and surely, there would be one if it were something serious. A week or two later, I found myself at the doctor's office for a routine visit. The doctor knew within seconds that something was wrong and that the "minor cold" was now in my baby's lungs. He was hooked up to oxygen while I sobbed, still not being able to recognize the wheezing sound that everyone else seemed to identify simply by looking at him.

Then, there was the time Lily fell off of a bunk bed, and I was 100 percent sure her wails were nothing more than a performance. Her arm didn't look broken in the least, and she's always been one to seek attention. Mother knows best, kid. Stop your crying! I gave her some Tylenol and put her to bed. When she woke up, her arm had swelled to twice its normal size and she couldn't move it without tears springing to her eyes. I'm quite sure that the only reason they started making obnoxiously fluorescent casts was to remind mothers like me just how poor our intuition can be. In my case, it was an eight-week reminder of how very much I sucked.

After nine years of motherhood, I still don't have that sixth sense concerning my children. I keep them home from school when it's clear an hour later that they simply didn't feel like going, and I send them with the sniffles only to have the school nurse instruct me to retrieve them shortly after drop off. It still doesn't dawn on me to feed them breakfast unless they ask for it and I never remember to tell them to hit the potty before we depart on road trips.

The good news is that, unlike when they were babies and the cries were indistinguishable, these days my kids tell me exactly what they need, when they need it. Lord knows, I need all the help I can get. The bad news? Now they never shut up.

# ★ Momfinitions ★

**MOMMY'S LAW:** The inevitable fact that only clean sheets will be wet, that fully snow-suited children will need to pee, and that the moment you sit down with a cup of coffee, all hell will break lose.

**MOMLUSIONAL:** Convincing oneself that the possibility of a restful sleep actually exists.

**MSP (MATERNAL SENSORY PERCEPTION):** Knowing from the very first ring of the phone that it's school calling to report a sick child.

**MOMFLEX:** The act of instinctively squeezing one's legs together while sneezing/coughing/laughing in an attempt to prevent inevitable bladder leakage.

**MOM SLEEVES:** Sleeves that have been rolled up to the elbow, to serve as tissues to snotty children.

**MOMSONIC HEARING:** Knowing exactly which child is coming down the stairs, based on their pace and stomp intensity.

**MOMPREHENSION:** The ability to perfectly comprehend multiple loud, obnoxious children competing to speak at the same exact time.

**MOMMY-TASKING:** The ability to do a hundred times more at once than a nonmother.

**MOMNESIA:** The act of forgetting where you put your keys, your sunglasses, your purse, your shoes, while simultaneously knowing the details of each child's schedule down to the minute.

**MOMPIPHANY:** The realization that you have no idea whatsoever what the hell you are doing.

## *Lie #2*

# YOU'LL BE BACK TO YOUR OLD SELF IN NO TIME

If I'd known what having children would do to my body, I'd have spent more time naked in high school. And I would have taken pictures.

*—Scary Mommy Confession #192319*

If "reclaiming your pre-baby body" were an answer on *Jeopardy*, the question would no doubt be "What is the unattainable myth that generation after generation of women fall prey to?"

Ladies, there's just no way around it, I'm sorry to say: You will *never* get your pre-baby body back. Ever.

Now, don't go ramming your minivan into a traffic pole or drowning yourself in seven pints of Ben & Jerry's. With a massive amount of effort and the blessing of genes that have the ability to bounce back from hell, it *is* possible to look decent after a baby. But even those freaks of nature who somehow manage to look *better* after children—even *those* women secretly hide the marks of pregnancy burned on their bodies forever. It's just the way it is.

Pre-baby-making-machine-transformation, shoes were the one thing I was willing to splurge on—my waist size may have fluctuated a bit due to how much drinking or eating out I was doing, but shoes seemed a wise investment. The perfect pair of sexy black heels. A gorgeous knee-high riding boot. Overpriced jeweled slip-ons that made me giddy with happiness every time I wore them. I loved them all and would frequently gaze at them in pure admiration. We had a happy life together. And then I had to go have a freaking baby.

I expected that my feet would swell during pregnancy, but what I didn't expect was that they would never return to their previous size. Weren't feet the one consistency I could count on in life? They're feet, for crying out loud—they're not supposed to grow after the age of eighteen. Or, they shouldn't at least. My leather and suede collection sat mocking me in my closet for years before I finally, tearfully passed them on to a childless cousin. I still cringe in shame every time I tell a shoe salesman my size.

Shoe sacrifice is the least of it, though. I have a friend with a knockout figure whose legs are so covered in varicose veins due to a blood disorder during pregnancy that she wears pants even when it's ninety degrees outside. Another has a frizzy mop on her head and constantly mourns the silky main she was lucky enough to have before her daughter's arrival, and yet another needs to manually tuck her muffin top into her pants like it's an undershirt.

Once you're a mom, you can look good, absolutely. But you

can never, *ever* reclaim exactly what you had before. It's a shame you probably didn't enjoy what you had, when you had it.

As if losing your flat stomach, perky boobs, and unfurrowed brow weren't enough, having children will also result in the loss of your mind. Sure, the lack of a fully functioning brain pales in comparison to tube-sock-shaped boobs, but it is pretty frustrating. Even worse, it never seems to go away.

For a while, I blamed my newfound flakiness on pregnancy brain. Later, it was the mindless routine of feeding and changing and burping a hundred times a day that resulted in my dumbness. After that, it was clearly just a side effect of listening to nothing but Laurie Berkner and the Wiggles. That shit would make anyone crazy! I made excuse after excuse after excuse. Eventually, though, it hit me: having children had not only ruined my body, it had also made me an idiot.

When Ben was a baby, I loaded him and Lily into the double stroller and hit the mall, ready to play the role of a mom who could successfully handle her two kids in public. I gave an Oscar-worthy performance all the way through the mall, buying things here and there, eating lunch at the food court, and even one-handedly changing a diaper in the Nordstrom restroom. So proud of myself, I trotted out the door, basking in the glow of a job well done. However, the smile washed off my face the minute I stepped into the parking lot and realized I had no idea *at all* where I had parked the car.

The kids were beginning to get fussy and I entered full-on freak-out mode. Nothing looked familiar, and I debated calling the cops and claiming the car was stolen. Instead, I flagged down security and the elderly guard drove us around for fifteen minutes searching for the "missing" car. Happens all the time, he assured me as he helped me out and wished me well. At the time, I was convinced he was just being kind, but since then I've seen a handful of other mothers being driven around in the security vans, babies obliviously bopping on their laps. The mall security escort is the walk of shame for mothers of young children.

And the list of flakiness goes on. We shout at our kids using the names of their siblings, we're incapable of finding our keys in less than ten minutes, and we never, ever remember what it is we got up off the couch to do in the first place. We've sacrificed our minds for our children, and sadly, they'll never remember us any other way. The good news? Eventually, we won't, either.

## ★ Requiem for a Mother's Body ★

Dearly Beloved,

We gather here today to pay our respects to the mind and body that used to live here—before motherhood. A mind and body that, sadly, was never appreciated until its untimely demise.

We remember those perky breasts previously so full of life and promise, now sucked dry of all hope and ambition.

We remember the blank canvas of the stomach that now looks more like the view of the Grand Canyon from fifteen thousand feet above.

We fondly recall the days when our vaginas were used for recreation rather than science experiments that have forever burned the words mucus and placenta and leukorrhea into our brains.

We remember how our asses used to defy gravity, and we lament how now they droop toward our thighs, forming some kind of wicked alliance against us.

We long for the days when a sneeze didn't equate to wet panties, and when exercising didn't require a completely empty bladder.

We mourn the loss of our favorite white pants, which we didn't actually lose but know will live for eternity in a plastic dry-cleaning bag hanging in the closet.

Above all, we vow to teach our daughters to savor and appreciate their undimpled flesh while they can. It won't look like that forever. We can prove it.

In the name of the good old days, let us all say, Amen.

## Lie #3

# MOTHERS HATE TO SEE
# THEIR CHILDREN SUFFER

I so love embarrassing my children. Now I know why
my mom always had that weird sneaky smile on her
face whenever my friends were around.

—*Scary Mommy Confession #252509*

I would gladly catch a violent stomach bug, if it spared my
child from the trauma of throwing up. I'd rather be the one
with the broken bone than have my child wear a cast. I'd take
the sore throat or poison ivy or seasonal allergies in a heartbeat if it spared any of my children the pain, suffering, or even
minor nuisance of any of them. Of course I would; I'm their
mother, and, as mothers, nothing is worse than seeing our children suffer.

Well, that's kind of true.

There is a special kind of suffering that *won't* pull at your
heartstrings, and you *won't* try to avoid at all costs. It's called pa-

★ 17 ★

rental embarrassment, my friends, and it's inevitable. No matter how hip you think you are, or how cool you try to be, that come a certain age, your child is bound to find you to be THE MOST EMBARRASSING CREATURE ON THE PLANET.

And if you're anything like me, you might just enjoy it.

Now it's worth noting at this point that the pain and suffering of parental embarrassment is a rite of passage. I have vivid memories of making my parents park blocks away from where they were dropping me off so they wouldn't be seen. I recall how I always opted to play at other kids' houses, because I could never guarantee that my mother wouldn't burst into song and do her best Ethel Merman impression while my friends and I played in my room. When I was twelve or thirteen, my parents could not have been more horrifying if they had skinned and eaten us for dinner.

Well, what goes around really does come around, because these days Lily is absolutely mortified by me. "Is *that* what you're wearing?" she asks as I descend the staircase looking, I think, pretty decent. She doesn't like the way I laugh, she doesn't like the way I wear my hair, and she HATES when I sing. She actually once asked me to change my shoes before her birthday party. This all from a child who thinks it's high fashion to wear gym shorts over leggings. I shudder to think of what her opinion of me will be in a few short years. The way I see it, I have two choices of how to deal with this: I can either be offended and try everything I can to become a parent who *doesn't* embarrass my offspring, or I can accept it.

Scratch that. There is a third choice we parents have when it comes to embarrassing our children, and that is to *embrace* it. Embrace it with pom-poms and cheers and glitter, because it turns out that embracing it is so unexpectedly fun.

Sometimes when I drop the kids off at school, I "forget" to do my hair and remove my slippers. Every now and then when I pick them up, I make a point of being early so that I can come to their classrooms and personally greet them, rather than wait for them to be escorted to my car. I tweeze my eyebrows in the car when I am stopped at red lights, especially when I'm chauffeuring around my kids' friends with them.

And that's just what I do now, when they are little. I have big plans for middle school. We have years of school trips for me to chaperone to look forward to. Public displays of affection and emotion at major milestones, like their bar and bat mitzvahs! Don't even get me started on proms and school dances!

I'm sure some people think this sort of behavior is unnecessary and maybe even cruel. But I figure I am just doing my part to keep the karma flowing. Besides, I'd argue that the ability to laugh at oneself is one of the most important traits a person can possess. It will serve them well in life and I'm simply getting my kids started early.

P.S.: Lily, Ben, and Evan, if you are reading this, please know that Mommy loves her little sheep so much! Hugs and kisses to the three kids with the cutest little tushies in the world!

# ★ Fun Tips for Mortifying Your Children ★

• Blast Broadway show tunes and belt out every last word, with the windows wide open.

• Send elaborate love letters in their lunch boxes.

• Chaperone field trips wearing a T-shirt bedazzled with your child's name.

• Bring pom-poms to sporting events and orchestrate a mommy cheer squad.

• Carry naked baby pictures everywhere and whip them out to complete strangers.

• Talk in made-up foreign accents to their friends.

• Do the Running Man, the Robot, and the Electric Slide when eighties music comes on in the grocery store.

• Use silly pet names in public. Loudly.

• Force them to wear matching knit sweaters for holiday photos.

• Label their clothing with smiley-faces and hearts around their names.

• Wipe their noses in front of their friends, applauding the contents.

• Welcome the bus wearing a bathrobe and slippers.

• Yell "I LOVE YOU!!!!" at the top of your lungs as they drive off for a playdate.

• Use saliva to wipe their dirty faces.

• Breathe.

## *Lie #4*
# IT TAKES A VILLAGE TO RAISE A CHILD

I invited you into my home as a guest. And you brought my two-year-old permanent markers and Play-Doh. Next time I visit you, I'm bringing your teenage daughter condoms and crack.

—*Scary Mommy Confession #80920*

On a crisp Sunday last October, our family went to a small carnival in a strip mall parking lot. It was a beautiful day, the money went to a good cause, and we knew the kids would have fun. Which they did, as Jeff and I glanced at our watches and snuck forbidden bites of cotton candy.

At one point, Ben excitedly ran up to me, grinning from ear to ear. I smiled back at my sweet boy, thrilled that he was having such a great time, until I saw the reason for his supreme happiness: a brand-new goldfish. Apparently he'd won it as a prize at one of the booths. And suddenly, without my consent, we were welcoming a new member to the family.

I ran over to the booth, planning to tell whichever teenager supervising the game where they could shove their goldfish. But to my horror, it wasn't some pimply-faced sixteen-year-old with a sick sense of humor. It was two mothers whom I knew from school, giddily handing out bags of fish to every kid who stepped up to the table. Mothers of other children. Mothers who know what bringing a fish into the house entails. They may as well have given my kids Ketel One and cigarettes, because that would have been a lot less offensive.

Is there any greater act of parental treason than gifting somebody else's kids with a goldfish?

One minute you are selflessly taking your children to a carnival—someplace you would gladly skip for a visit to the gynecologist—and the next, you're a pet owner. A pet that *you* will have to feed, whose water *you* will have to change, and whose imminent death will force you to have "the conversation" with your innocent children far sooner than you are ready.

Whatever happened to "It takes a village"?! Aren't we parents supposed to *help* raise one another's kids, not make it harder?

You know how when you have a baby, the nurse has to physically escort you out to the car and supervise you putting your newborn into the car seat? Well, there should be another law that also requires new mothers to recite an oath of allegiance to all other mothers before they let you pull away: *I solemnly swear to always be on team mommy, to never give your kids anything I wouldn't want you to give mine, to do my best to help you get six hours of sleep each night and at least three solo showers a week, and to never, ever, under any circumstances, give your child a fish. Amen.*

As mothers of daughters, you'd think we'd all be on the same side—the side prolonging our daughters' innocence for as long as possible. What's with the moms who let their third-grade daughters dress like whores? Call me a prude, but I think Daisy Duke shorts, flimsy tank tops, and sandals with heels are a little much for a nine-year-old. My rule of thumb: if you don't know what a labia is, then you shouldn't wear clothes that expose yours to the rest of us. Look, I respect your right to choose what your kids wear, at least in theory. But if your daughter dresses like a slut, then mine will want to as well. And that's when I start to hate you.

And don't get me started on the parents who moonlight as the rich tooth fairy. Ben came home from school one day with a baby tooth in hand. *Look what I lost today,* he squealed. *I'm gonna be rich!* Apparently one of his friends came into school that day with a crisp ten-dollar bill from the tooth fairy. For one tooth! We have three children, and last I counted they each had thirty-two teeth. There is no way I am spending nearly ONE THOUSAND DOLLARS on their rotten teeth—and that's *before* orthodontics!

The list of things parents do to make raising children harder for the rest of us goes on and on. There are the parents who do a half-assed job of shampooing lice out of their own kids' hair. The parents who buy their kids the hot new toy the day it hits the shelves. The parents who throw birthday parties that rival wedding receptions. If I could, I'd gather all of those parents in one room and become the parent who goes Nightmare on Elm Street on their asses.

Of course, I'm also surrounded by wonderful friends and family without whom I wouldn't stay sane. The ones who offer to pick my kid up from school when I'm out of town. The ones who provide my kids with after-school snacks when I forgot to pack any. My mother, who folds my laundry when I'm just about to burn it all and start over. But just when I think I've found my village, someone goes and gives my kid a freaking fish.

I suppose, though, it should be expected. After all, every village has its resident idiot.

# ★ Decoding Mom-Speak ★

| | |
|---|---|
| Oh dear, (s)he's quite a character! | Your kid is a brat. |
| It's adorable that you let him dress himself! | I would never let my child look so ridiculous. |
| You're glowing! | OMG, you've gotten so fat! |
| Have you lost weight? | You look like hell, but I'm trying to think of something nice to say. |
| I love what you've done with your hair! | Oh look, you showered today! |
| Your husband is so lucky to have you. | And I'm so glad I wasn't the one to marry him. |
| I'm so glad you came by for a visit! | Please get out of my house and CALL next time, you rude bitch. |
| I'll let you know. | Over my dead body. |
| Oh, isn't he darling! | I'm never watching that child for you. |
| I promise, you'll be okay. | You're screwed. |

## Lie #5

# HAVING KIDS KEEPS
# YOU YOUNG

I put salt in my coffee this morning. My hair is un-
washed. I haven't slept in two years. I regularly injure
myself on small plastic objects. I envy my pets' daily
routine. I depend on caffeine and *Sesame Street*. I.
Am. Mom.

—*Scary Mommy Confession* #127336

I read an article a few years ago about a gorgeous and slender movie star in her late forties. When she was asked about her secrets for looking so young, flawless, and vibrant, her answer was simple: "My kids keep me young," she chirped. "I'm always playing with them and running around after them and it has taken *years* off of my appearance." It's a good thing the magazine was in print and I wasn't in a live studio audience at some talk show, because if that woman had uttered such foolishness in front of me, I would not have been able to restrain myself from physically attacking her. Lady: Your kids are not to thank for your flawless appearance, your plastic surgeon is. And you're not fooling anyone.

Whoever first uttered the phrase "children keep you young" clearly didn't have children themselves. Because once you have kids, you know better. Children don't keep you young; they prematurely age the hell out of you.

I can't say with absolute certainty that the increasing frequency with which I have to color my hair is directly related to having children, but don't you think it's suspicious that the gray hairs on my head seem to appear in two-year increments? I don't have scientific proof that the wrinkles on my forehead become more pronounced every year on each of my kids' birthdays, but it sure seems like a trend to me. And while I expected that giving birth vaginally three times in four years would, um, loosen things up, I didn't expect that at thirty-five years old I would be watching commercials for Depends with sincere curiosity.

Speaking of television commercials, what's with all the advertisements that show gleeful mothers playfully chasing their children around the yard?

The last time I chased my own kids, it was to retrieve my phone from an untimely death in a stream. And I *definitely* wasn't laughing about it. I had a moment last summer when I thought that maybe I was uniquely lazy, that perhaps other mothers did play chase with their kids. I was inside the house, watching through the window as my forty-something cousin chased after her ten-year-old son. Boy, I thought to myself. She is so *playful*. Such a fun mom! Just as I was starting to put on my sneakers out of mommy guilt, I watched as she caught up to him, ordered him to open his hand, and snatched a stolen piece of candy out of his grubby paws. She wasn't chasing after him. She was literally *chasing* him.

Running around after kids isn't a job for parents. It's for the other people who don't live with the little suckers.

Take my brother and sister-in-law, for instance. They are a mere three years younger than Jeff and I, but when they're around the kids, you'd swear we were separated by generations. They dart around playing chase for hours. They have the stamina and patience for endless games of Simon Says and Red Rover and Marco Polo. And I'm not talking the lazy mom versions that I play here and there ("Simon says fetch Mommy a Diet Coke and we'll play later!") but full-on games. Endlessly. They giggle and skip and dance and somersault while Jeff and I look on with food dribbling from our chins and glazed expressions on our wrinkled, crusty faces. We'll just let you enjoy the kids, we say. It's not because we *don't* want to go for that three-mile hike, but because we literally can't. Once we have family in town to entertain the kids, we're too fucking exhausted to even think about moving.

Before we had children, family visits were a time to show off our wonderful life together. We'd parade our childless or empty-nester guests around town, eating at the yummy restaurants we frequented and cooking them feasts at home. I'd have candles lit in the guest bath and an array of travel-size shampoos and conditioners waiting in the shower. Clean towels sat at the foot of the bed, and my guests could find their favorite beverages lining the fridge. Their wish was my command, and I made it my mission to make their weekend away as relaxing and enjoyable as possible. These days? My mission is to relinquish all parental responsibility and get a good nap under my belt while they earn their keep.

We offer our guests a quick tour: where to find clean(ish) towels, what food is still safe to eat, and which bathroom to avoid due to the permanent stench of little-boy piss. Then Jeff and I dart up the stairs to our bedroom, before our guests know what hit them. *You're fine with them, right?* we call after them, not waiting around for an answer. *They can handle themselves . . . we think.* By the time the weekend is over, our guests look like they've been through war. Suddenly they've acquired new wrinkles, and the light in their eyes seems to have extinguished. But I don't feel badly. After all, they get to return home to a childless utopia and regain that youthful glow we kissed goodbye with our firstborn.

So, no, having kids doesn't keep you young. It does, however, serve as excellent birth control for your luminous and rested childless family and friends. Compared to us parents, they look and feel as if they've bathed in the fountain of youth. Or, perhaps that's just all the sex they're still having.

Either way, they're assholes.

# ★ Scary Mommy's Rules of the Playground ★

**1.** I will not push you endlessly on the swing. If you want to swing, pump.

**2.** I will not swing from bars. I am not a monkey.

**3.** I do not go down slides (for fear of my ass getting stuck midway).

**4.** We are not playmates. At the playground, I have my friends and you have yours.

**5.** Stay away from sandboxes at all costs. This isn't a beach.

**6.** Hide-and-seek anywhere but home isn't fun for mommy. Don't even think about it.

**7.** There is no need to yell "LOOK AT ME!!!" every three seconds. I'm (half) watching. And if I miss that particular slide dismount, I'll catch the next one.

**8.** Don't ask me to play on the seesaw. I don't need to be reminded that I weigh more than all of you combined.

**9.** Don't tell me you are bored. I guarantee you'll be more bored at home.

**10.** Don't do anything that will result in an ER visit. Or we may never come back.

*Lie #6*

# PARENTS WOULDN'T DREAM OF HURTING THEIR CHILDREN

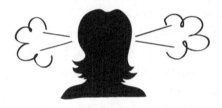

I have been spit on, smacked around, kicked until I was bruised, my hair pulled out. I need to come forward and speak out. I, too, am a victim of toddler abuse.

—*Scary Mommy Confession # 253360*

Once upon a time I was the mother to a single baby, and my life revolved around her and her alone. Mommy and Me classes. The library. The park. Baby ballet. My heart swelled with her little accomplishments and I could feel it breaking when she hurt in any way.

When my precious sweetheart was around six months old or so, there was a story in the local news about a mother physically abusing her child. Those sort of stories pulled at my heartstrings before, but since becoming a mother, they made me physically ill. I was horrified and called my own mother in a complete outrage. What kind of mother could ever dream of causing harm to her precious offspring, I shouted. How could this be? And then my mother said something I'll never forget. It was the moment that left me questioning everything I knew about her—as a mother, as a grandmother, and, frankly, as a human being.

*The only thing separating the women who do those awful things from those who don't is impulse control. Everyone has the urge to hurt their children at some time or another; most people just have the intelligence and restraint to walk away.*

She could have told me that I was adopted and that Bill Cosby was my real father, and I would have been less shocked. Who was this woman, and did she really just admit to having the urge to harm me?

My mom laughed at my horror and assured me that one day I would understand. But for the next two years, I was undeterred. Every time I recalled that conversation I felt a sense of pride that I still couldn't relate to that feeling she warned me about. In my mind, it was just one more affirmation that I was a better mother. *Obviously.*

And then Lily turned three.

I'm not sure who coined the phrase "the terrible twos," but they mustn't have been a parent because two wasn't all that terrible. Lily was sweet, easy, and totally welcoming to her new baby brother. Our days were a joy and the worst thing I ever wanted to do to her was dress her up as a flower and pretend to be Anne Geddes.

Once she turned three, though, everything changed. I think it was around that time that I officially became a Scary Mommy. It was like a switch was flipped and my precious baby girl turned into Satan. And I became that mother I never imagined

I could be. The mother who could think about hurting her own child.

The first time it happened, Lily was going on hour two of a tantrum over Lemon Heads. She wanted the entire box of candy, and I wouldn't allow it. (Side note: Really, Lily?! Lemon heads? Candy isn't worth getting cut over unless it's filled with chocolate.) After fifteen minutes, I was ready to cave but held my ground on principle. She wailed like her life was ending and in the process, she woke her napping brother. Suddenly I had two screaming children; plus my husband was out of town and I hadn't had adult interaction in three days. As she went on and on and on, I had a fleeting urge to throw her against the wall. *Throw her against the wall!* It was a terrifying feeling. I felt so out of control, so vulnerable. It scared the shit out of me.

And then came a rush of that intelligence and restraint my mom spoke of. I put Ben in his crib, soothed my screaming Lily into the nap she desperately needed, and sat on the front stoop catching my breath. It was the first of many defining motherhood moments for me, as I made a conscious decision about the kind of mother I wanted to be.

With three kids now, ages five, seven, and nine, I sometimes have momentary rages. Oh, who am I kidding? I have those urges *all the time*. But being a Scary Mommy is in part about knowing how to separate fantasy from reality. We might think like crazy women sometimes, but we love our kids and would never, ever hurt them.

But a girl can dream.

# ★ Ten Things Every Mother Needs ★

**1.** A strong gag reflex

**2.** Deep coffee mugs

**3.** Deeper wineglasses

**4.** Concealer in the perfect shade

**5.** Extra-strength Advil

**6.** Purell

**7.** At least one room with a lock on it

**8.** A pair of perfect black yoga pants

**9.** Mr. Clean Magic Erasers

**10.** A sense of humor. A big one.

## *Lie #7*
# PARENTING STRENGTHENS A MARRIAGE

Every now and then, when I wake up and look at my husband I think, Well, I can either make him breakfast, or beat him to death with the pan.

—*Scary Mommy Confession #202999*

Before I had my daughter, I heard from friend after friend that having a baby brought them closer to their spouses. That seeing the person they chose to spend the rest of their life with caring for their baby made a strong marriage even stronger. That they were more in synch, more in love, and more committed to one another than ever.

ARE YOU FUCKING KIDDING ME??? I wanted to yell to those so-called friends at three o'clock in the morning while attempting to feed a crying baby and simultaneously listening to my husband snoring peacefully in the next room. *This* makes for a stronger marriage?!? Bullshit, it does.

The very fact that a woman is built to carry and nurse a child ALL BY HERSELF should be enough of a sign that marriage is not meant to survive parenthood. A man's sole role in baby-making is an orgasm. Literally the best feeling in the world, and poof! He's done. We, on the other hand, have to suffer through nine months of bloody, mucousy, *National Geographic*–style hell. And, then, as if that hell weren't bad enough, we're the ones who have only two very bad options: pushing out a creature the size of a watermelon from a hole the size of a baby carrot *or* undergoing major surgery. What are the men doing at this point? Watching. And possibly even smoking a celebratory cigar.

If there were any justice at all in parenting, mothers' jobs would be done once the baby is born. Our husbands would turn to us with empathetic, admiring eyes and say, "You've done enough. Please, I'll take it from here. Forever."

But that's not how it works. As if our ruined vaginas were not sacrifice enough, our boobs become the next casualty in the Battle of Formerly Desirable Body Parts. Suddenly we're lactating at the sound of random crying babies, suffering from painfully raw nipples, and literally spilling out of our maternity bras.

To add salt to the open wound, we get only six weeks—six?!—to heal before our husbands start nagging us for sex again, which is *exactly* what got us into trouble in the first place and the *last* thing on earth we feel like doing.

I swear, it's a miracle any couple survives the first six weeks of parenthood! First the good news: While it might not feel that way at the time, there will come a point when you *do* want to have (PROTECTED, FOR THE LOVE OF GOD!) sex again with your husband. Your vagina will heal, you will no longer live in fear of spraying him with breast milk, and, at the end of the day, you're just going to want to feel like a woman again. So here's the bad news: your children will make it their mission in life to prevent that from happening.

Welcome to every child's most favorite sport: cock-blocking their mothers. Maybe it has to do with the whole Oedipal complex. Maybe subconsciously they don't want another sibling. Maybe they're simply programmed that way. All I know is that my children thrive on getting in the way of my sex life and there's nothing to kill the mood like two sets of little eyes peering at me from the doorway. There is, actually. It's the memory of those little eyes staring at me and, sadly, the image is burned in my brain. Seems it's burned into theirs as well, since they bring it up frequently to people like my father. Now *that* was a fun dinner table discussion.

But, it doesn't end with sex, or lack thereof. Before we became parents, I don't think I fully appreciated just how much my husband enjoyed doing absolutely nothing. I suppose because I enjoyed it, too, and we had the luxury of sleeping away an entire Saturday if we wanted to. We'd lounge around in bed until well after noon, head to brunch, come home, and nap again, before heading out for the evening. It was gluttonous, selfish, and absolutely amazing.

Sadly, those days ended abruptly the moment we had children. Well, they did for me, at least. "I need my sleep!" my husband cries when I awaken him after I've been dealing with the kids for a few hours already. "You can operate without eight hours a night and I can't!" No, sweetheart, it's not that. I have no choice in the matter. If I slept as late as my heart desired, the children would tear apart the house and we'd find ourselves toilet-papered to the bed surrounded by wild beasts high on a breakfast of Lucky Charm marshmallows and chocolate milk.

Surviving coparenting requires a love that is rock solid. Between the clashing of differing discipline styles and moral beliefs and dealing with once mildly annoying habits that would now be cause for justifiable homicide, you need it. I don't view anniversaries as milestones; I see them as miracles. Pop open the champagne and celebrate: you've done the (almost) impossible!

As for those friends of mine who claimed parenthood would make my marriage stronger, I'd really like to call them up and scream at them for telling me such lies. I'll ask them why they hate me so much, why they take pleasure in my pain. I'll swear to them that I'll never do to anyone else what they have done to me.

I won't really, though. I heard half of them got divorced.

# ★ An Ode to My Husband, ★

## INSPIRED BY GO THE FUCK TO SLEEP

*The dishes are washed, everything tidy in its place.*
*The leftovers boxed up, my dear, and the counters wiped clean.*
*I've asked you six times, don't make me say it again,*
*Please, for the love of God,*
*Just empty the fucking trash can.*

*You work hard and need your rest,*
*I do know that and care . . .*
*But you slept all night and napped three times,*
*You've more than gotten your share,*
*It's time to awake and get on with the day.*
*Wake the fuck up already, you hear me okay?*

*You've been flipping for an hour,*
*But have yet to pick a show.*
*Could you be more annoying?*
*It seems the answer is no.*
*Surrender the remote, I'll ask one last time,*
*Or I'm kicking you out, right on your behind.*

*The day is getting dim,*
*Soon it will be night.*
*I can't see a thing, my love,*
*You have to know I'm right.*
*I'm not as tall as you, so I need your larger height.*
*Would it kill you to change that fucking hall light?*

*I know you feel sick but I do as well.*
*My nose is stuffy, too,*
*And my throat sore as hell.*
*Please stop complaining.*
*It's just a little cold.*
*So shut up and cope,*
*You're not that fucking old.*

*I love you so much.*
*I value what you say.*
*But now I'm trying to sleep,*
*And you're keeping me awake.*
*For the last time, my sweet,*
*I just don't give a crap.*
*Enough already, really,*
*Just shut your damn pie trap.*

*I'm lying in bed, desperately needing my rest.*
*You've been sleeping for hours,*
*Happily passed out on your chest.*
*How are you so loud, I really don't know.*
*But if you don't fucking stop snoring,*
*You're gonna have to go.*

*Is this too much to ask*
*From the man I adore?*
*I really don't get why I'm so easy to ignore.*
*Start listening to me, that's all there is to it.*
*Oh, and the dog needs a walk.*
*Just fucking do it.*

*Lie #8*

# YOU'RE THE GROWN-UP

I beat my kids at Super Mario Bros. and proceeded to
do a victory dance that made them all cry. Whoops.

—*Scary Mommy Confession #254143*

There is this girl I know who just brings out the worst in me. She makes me act petty and competitive and judgmental. I don't know if it's the look of superiority on her face, the callous and bossy way she treats her friends, or her flagrant disregard for other people's feelings, but I cringe every time I see her.

And she knows it.

I can see that my disdainful stares make her a little uncomfortable. I can tell that she tries to avoid me, often going a roundabout way just so she doesn't have to come face-to-face with me in the hallway. And I suspect she comes home from school every day and complains to her mother and father about "Lily's mother" making mean faces at her.

Yes, I'm talking about a nine-year-old girl. And I just can't help myself.

It started one Saturday several years ago, when Lily called friend after friend to see about a playdate. To her dismay, no one was available and they all had the same excuse: "I'm going to 'Paige's' birthday party." *Why wasn't I invited to Paige's birthday party,* Lily cried to me. *Why doesn't she like me?*

Now the mature thing to do would have been to explain to Lily that not everyone needs to be friends with everyone else, that that's the way life works, and that it wasn't a big deal. And I did that. I told her all of those things and more. I was so convincing that, to this day two full years later, Lily *still* tries to be this girl's friend, despite coming home at least twice a week complaining about something Paige said to her that hurt her feelings. I'm impressed with how mature Lily is about the situation. Despite the rocky relationship, Lily still seems interested in a genuine friendship with Paige.

Me, on the other hand? I'm ready to take that bitch down.

I *may* have spent the entire two hours as a class helper a few months back shooting daggers at Paige from across the room. There is a *slight* chance I talked Lily out of inviting Paige to her own birthday party last year—the one that every other girl in the class attended. And I can't say with *total* sincerity that I was sorry to hear about a minor injury she sustained on the playground at recess.

I know. I am going straight to hell. I'm supposed to be the grown-up, and here I am bullying a third grader. But the truth is, sometimes we parents behave more childishly than our own kids.

I frequently find myself in this situation with Lily, with whom I sometimes feel like I am on a playdate gone wrong. You know the kind: we start off great, playing nicely and enjoying our time together, and then about fifty minutes in the mood changes, we start to argue about nothing and we end up on opposite sides of the house, pouting about the other's bossiness. I don't know what it is about tween girls that make mothers act like bitchy schoolgirls, but it's a phenomenon that scientists should study.

A few months back, I went to visit my brother and his fiancée in Seattle. As a special treat, I invited eight-year-old Lily to come with me, as I thought we could both use the time together without Jeff and the boys. Big mistake. We spent the six-hour flight out there fighting and the six-hour flight home not speaking to each other. And the three days in between weren't that much better. Needless to say, I was beyond thrilled to get home and see my mama's boys who still think I shit rainbows. Jeff, on the other hand, wasn't as happy to see us.

"Can you two please go back to Seattle," he hissed at Lily and me as we bickered that first night home about I don't even know what. "It was so peaceful here without you two." That's saying a lot, considering he was home alone with a four-year-old bruiser who breaks everything he touches, a six-year-old boy who speaks so loudly you would think he swallowed a microphone for breakfast, and a ten-week-old golden retriever puppy who acts like a ten-week-old golden retriever puppy.

It's not just my relationships with Lily and her frenemies that bring out the child in me. There's the movie *Girls Just Wanna Have Fun*, which I watch several times a month because God knows I should have been on a teen dance competition in my youth. Then there's *Victorious,* my favorite show on television, and of course the *Victorious* feature-length special. It's ironic that Lily and I can have so much trouble getting along, since we have the same taste in movies and television.

My husband is no better. If the IRS knew the man who claims "head of household" status on our tax returns, they would laugh their asses off. First of all, he likes *Victorious,* too. And by "likes" it, I mean he watches it on the DVR. Second, he is afraid of the dark. Well, not the dark really, but the man does check closets before bedtime to make sure no one is hiding in them. And then of course there is his fondness for chocolate milk. Have you ever seen the expression on a waitress's face when a grown man orders chocolate milk? I do. Weekly.

I suppose all parents are just big kids playing the role of responsible adult most of the time. Sure, our daily obligations help suppress our inner child, but we all have moments of regression. And I'm thankful for that, because sometimes being a grown-up can really suck.

## ★ I'll hate your kid forever if . . . ★

- S(he) gets my kid sick before a family vacation.

- S(he) ruins my kid's birthday party.

- S(he) is the reason I am taking my kid to the ER.

- S(he) makes fun of something I love about my child.

- S(he) hurts my dog. (Hello, psychopath.)

- S(he) cuts my kid's hair.

- S(he) bullies my kid.

- S(he) gives my kid lice.

- S(he) password protects my electronics and doesn't share the password.

- S(he) picks my kid last for the sports team.

## Lie #9

# YOU'LL GET MORE SLEEP WHEN THEY ARE OLDER

In the shopping center today, I nearly dropped my six-year-old off at the lost-children sign and pretended he wasn't mine. I know how bad that sounds, but his attitude was THAT BAD. And I am THAT TIRED.

*—Scary Mommy Confession #250762*

Ask any mother of a newborn what the hardest part of having a baby is, and I bet she'll tell you it's the sleep deprivation. Sure, it's true that babies do little more than sleep, eat, and poop. The problem, though, is that they do those things in two-hour increments. It's as if they can't tell time or something.

I remember hearing over and over again that I should "sleep while the baby sleeps," which, frankly, is a lot better in theory than in practice. In fact, it may very well be the least useful piece of advice in the history of useless pieces of advice. If all mothers slept while their babies slept, the world would come to a screeching halt. Laundry wouldn't get done. Email would go unanswered. People would starve! I learned early on with my first newborn that sleep is simply one of the first in a long list of sacrifices you make for your children.

And I didn't mind, because I was assured that I would get more sleep once my kids got older. Now, I should have known better than to believe this lie, since it was coming from the same people who told me that parenting strengthens a marriage and that I'd be back to my old self in no time. But here I am with three kids, ages five, seven, and nine, and I think I get *less* sleep today than I did when they were babies.

There are many things for which I have little patience where my children are concerned. The fact that I have to bribe them with dessert in order to get them to eat protein and vegetables, for instance. Or the way they carry on as if they were the Linda Blair character in *The Exorcist* when I want them to take medicine that will make them feel a thousand times better. Or that they can build towers with perfect precision, yet are incapable of aiming into the toilet.

But what drives me the most insane is their refusal to sleep. Putting my children to bed is a two-hour ordeal that I start dreading from the moment I awake in the morning. If stalling at bedtime were an Olympic sport, my kids would be on the cover of *Sports Illustrated*. One would think they were forced to sleep on wooden slats in the freezing rain rather than on plush mattresses with high-thread-count sheets in their very own rooms, based on the way they carry on. They whine and bargain and beg for a few more minutes of playtime while I roll my eyes and question their sanity. *Don't they know that I would kill to be tucked in with a story and a kiss by 8:30 p.m.?* If I were a cold bitch I would tell them that life doesn't get any better than this and that they should get a good night's rest while they can.

Once they finally fall asleep—usually around 9:30 or 10:00 in our house—I have the opportunity to grab about three hours of sleep myself. Most nights, though, I have too much to do, and this is my first bit of me time all day. So more often than not, I head back downstairs and cuddle with my laptop instead of my husband for a few hours.

Like clockwork, just as I am ready to call it a day and head to bed, one of my kids will reappear. If it's Evan, he's probably wet himself. So that means a quick shower, which by the way he forces me to take with him. So it's midnight and I'm washing my hair. Might as well shave my legs while I'm in there, right? By the time we dry off and I get Evan into clean pajamas, Ben stumbles into my room. "I had a bad dream," he whines, as he climbs into my bed. Somehow, Jeff remains asleep during all of this commotion, happily snoring my sanity away.

Finally, I'm in bed. The good news is I don't have to wash my hair in the morning. The bad news is Evan and Ben think it's *already* morning. They beg to watch a television show. They ask if they can have cereal. Evan begins to ask questions about my belly fat, and Ben, who is lying there with his head on my shoulder, closely inspecting my face, wonders why my nostrils are so big.

After about forty-five minutes, the questions stop and the boys fall back asleep. And just as I doze off to fantasies of Ryan Gosling's abs, Lily comes barreling down from her room in a mad dash for the bathroom. She flips on all the lights, slams the toilet seat down, and, if I'm lucky, finds her way into our bedroom as well. Of course, she needs to nudge and kick her brothers on her way into the bed, setting off a forty-five-minute session of extreme whining.

"Lily has more room than me."

"Ben won't stop kicking me!"

"Evan, did you just wet yourself . . . again?"

It's two in the morning before I finally fall asleep for good, usually in some kind of awkward position that will require the services of a chiropractor. And then just as Ryan Gosling is getting ready to lift me in the air *Dirty Dancing*–style, Jeff's alarm goes off and our day begins.

So, no, in my experience neither children nor mothers sleep better as kids age. I would argue it gets worse. I'm hoping that I'll finally get some rest when my kids leave for college. Although I hear that when menopause hits it wreaks havoc on your sleeping all over again.

Of course it does.

# ★ Perks to Being Awake When ★ the Rest of the World Sleeps

**1.** You can empty out your inbox without it immediately filling back up.

**2.** You can fold and put away every last piece of laundry without a child depositing a filthy article of clothing in the prized empty hamper.

**3.** You can do all the dishes and the sink will remain empty for hours.

**4.** You can eat whatever you want, without begging hands suddenly wanting a taste.

**5.** You can take a long shower, with all the hot water you want.

**6.** You can drink a glass of water, without a child depositing backwash into it.

**7.** You can mop the floors and admire them, as they remain gloriously footprint-free, for at least two hours.

**8.** You can watch anything you want on TV.

**9.** You can clip your nails or pluck your eyebrows or do a face mask or shave your legs without an audience.

**10.** You can pee in peace.

## Lie #10

# MOTHERS LOVE COOKING FOR THEIR KIDS

Today, as I was pressed for time, I heated a frozen Stouffer's lasagna for dinner. When my children were served, they yelled, "This is the best dinner you've ever made!" I cook healthy, balanced meals every day.

*—Scary Mommy Confession #258590*

As a wife, I fully subscribe to the theory that the way to a man's heart is through his stomach. Though I may suck at many other wifely duties, at the very least, my man never goes hungry. Eggplant parmesan, lasagna, roasted chicken and potatoes, pulled barbeque pork . . . I know what my husband likes to dine on, and it makes me happy to cook those things for him. Just call me Donna Reed and slap an apron on me!

Unfortunately, the same does not hold true for my children. Happiness is the last thing I feel when feeding them these days. Frustration? Check. Annoyance? Check. Impatience? Check.

Rage? Yes, sometimes, check. But, it's been a while since I got much satisfaction from nourishing those growing bellies.

Once upon a time, when the three of them were tiny babies, I did get pleasure from the act of feeding them. Just the two of us, curled up in a rocking chair, oblivious to the rest of the world. There's simply no other feeling in the world like being solely responsible for the nourishment of a helpless little newborn. But then they have to go and start solid foods and mess the whole thing up.

You know the face that babies make when they taste their first morsel of real food, whether it be peas, squash, or sweet potatoes? It's a combination of disgust at the unfamiliar flavor and shock and awe that the person they love most in the world would expose them to such horror. Well, that's pretty much the face my children make each and every night when I answer the dreaded question, "Mommy, what's for dinner?"

There are a mere four things I could say that would illicit a response of "Yum!" or "When will it be ready?!" from all of my kids: pizza (delivery only, never homemade), breakfast for dinner, chicken fingers, or macaroni and cheese. And that's it. I mean, that's not *all* my kids ever eat, but that's all they eat happily.

When I cook anything other than those things or, God forbid, something new that they've never before had, the response from the peanut gallery is one of dry heaving, wailing, or flat-out refusal to eat. I find myself bribing them with dessert if they even eat junk for dinner. "Eat three more bites of this meatball and you can have some ice cream," I beg. "Pleaaaaase . . . just a little more sesame chicken and rice and then you can have your cookies?" I wish they could understand how ridiculous it is.

Lunches aren't much better. Every morning, I hastily slap cream cheese on some bagels or smear some peanut butter and jelly on some slices of bread, throw an applesauce and bag of pretzels into their lunch boxes, and call it a day. Last year, Jeff had the audacity to offer his commentary on my process. "You're not making those sandwiches with much love," he snidely remarked, as I plopped the jelly down, assembly-line-style, on six slices of bread.

And then I killed him. Butter knife straight to the heart.

Gee, Jeff, I'm not sure where my enthusiasm for making our children their crappy lunches went. Perhaps I lost it the six millionth time I smeared that cream cheese. Regardless, love has nothing to do with it. I choose to show my love for my children a billion other ways. Their lunches is not one of them.

Love wasn't the secret ingredient in Jeff's dinner that night, either, unless Papa John's uses a dash of love along with their special sauce, as I retaliated for his unwanted opinion by providing cold pizza for dinner. But at least the kids ate that night, and I got a night off from cooking, which makes me even happier than presenting my man with a delicious, home cooked meal of his liking.

Even Donna Reed needs a night off.

# ★ Things Kids Never Say ★

**1.** You're making what for dinner? YUM!

**2.** I know where my soccer cleats are!

**3.** I'm going to play with my toys now. I really do have so many of them.

**4.** Mommy is on the phone right now, so let's entertain ourselves quietly.

**5.** That puddle would make an awfully big mess. I'm not going to stomp in it.

**6.** We're going to be in the car for five hours? Let me pee first.

**7.** I'm too full for dessert.

**8.** I have a lot of homework tonight, I should get started.

**9.** Can I have some dental floss?

**10.** We all decided that we want to watch the same thing on TV.

**11.** We're going to be late, let's go!

**12.** You're so much more fun than Daddy.

**13.** Let's get those thank-you notes over with!

**14.** I've had enough electronics for the day.

**15.** I have a class project due two weeks from now.

**16.** I'm ready for bed.

**17.** I don't care what my friends are allowed to have or do.

**18.** What did you ask me to do before? I want to make sure I go and do it.

**19.** I'm really enjoying this long car ride.

**20.** I need to wash my hands.

**21.** I'll take the smallest piece, please.

**22.** You're in the bathroom? Okay, I'll wait to ask you my unimportant question.

**23.** We don't have school tomorrow? That stinks.

**24.** There's so much to do in this house!

**25.** Thank you for that yummy lunch! I didn't trade any of it at the cafeteria.

## *Lie* #11
# YOU ARE YOUR OWN HARSHEST CRITIC

Having a teenager in the house has been detrimental to my self-esteem. Sometimes, I want to treat her exactly the way she treats me, but that would be child abuse.

*—Scary Mommy Confession #252463*

I'm a horrible mother. My kids watch too much television, they eat too much junk food, and they don't participate in enough extracurricular activities. They have poor sleeping habits because Jeff and I were too lazy to put them to bed properly when we had our chance, and sometimes they wear shorts in November.

I'm a shitty wife. I'm always cranky and frequently take it out on my husband. I reserve my few moments of pleasantness for my kids, and so all my husband gets is "No," "Are you kidding me?!" and "Do what I said." Sex these days is like a drive-in movie: open for your viewing pleasure, but you're on your own.

I'm so fat. I need a tummy tuck, and my upper arms have a better sense of movement than my feet. I vacillate between three different clothing sizes. And by vacillate, I mean I ONCE hit the smaller of the three in the last nine years.

I can't even count the number of times that thoughts like this have raced through my head. I'm a mother, a wife, and my own person, but it's rare that I am satisfied with my performance in one area, let alone all three. My failures seem so obvious—I assume everyone must think the same of me. Strangely, though, every time I've ever voiced these feelings, I've been told the same thing: I'm too hard on myself. I'm my own worst critic.

This, my friends, is one of the most pervasive and pernicious lies of motherhood. I've said it, you've said it, and it's just plain bullshit.

There is nobody harder on a mom than her fellow mother. It starts bright and early with pregnancy. As if the symptoms you're suffering weren't bad enough, when you are expecting, everyone's mission becomes to knock you down. Not literally, of course, because that would be attempted manslaughter, but they will try to knock you down nonetheless. They will insult your appearance, question your choice of lunch meat, and casually note just how much weight you have gained.

Once the baby comes, it's like you've signed on a dotted line agreeing to put every decision you make into the public domain for open critique. Your baby's name, your decision to breastfeed or *not* to breastfeed, the sleep habits you're enforcing . . . everything is simply an opportunity for people to stick their noses in your business and judge away like it's a spectator sport.

And that's just what we say to each other's faces. The

behind-the-back talk is even harsher. But because we're mothers, we find a way to mask our judgment in feigned concern and helpfulness.

We once lived in a neighborhood where, on the first night under our new roof, the queen bee of the subdivision gave us an illustrated list (I kid you not) of our surrounding neighbors. Each house had a little notation next to their name: #2703 hosts the Easter egg hunts and fights loudly; #2708 are going through a divorce, but it's amicable; #2714 babysits, has a Fourth of July bash, but passed lice around to the whole Girl Scout troop. As she walked in with her tray of brownies and neon nails, I wondered what notes she was taking at my place. #2601: Appears not to have showered in three days, bottle-feeds her infant, and lets the older one watch too much TV—SHITTY MOTHER, her note likely screamed.

Unfortunately, the critiquing doesn't end with other mothers. Kids can be just as brutal, especially our own. I'll be innocently showering first thing in the morning when a midget body will barge into the bathroom, and upon seeing my figure in the shower, run out screaming, like I have scarred him or her for life. It's not uncommon for the child, whoever it is, to fall into a fit of giggles and call for his siblings. "Lily! Evan! Ben! Mommy is naaaaakkked. Come see!!" If I'm *really* lucky, all three will stand outside the shower pointing and laughing like I'm a zoo animal taking a dump.

Once I get out of the shower, time permitting, I slather myself in lotion. Should I be lucky enough to have an audience, they will inevitably point to my thighs. "What's that purple squiggle, Mommy?" A spider vein, I sigh. "That one, too?" Yes, that one, too, honey. "Over here, too?" Yes, my darling, that's what they're called. Let's move on.

"Okay. What's this?"

It's a stretch mark. That's a scar. That's a vein. That's cellulite. That's hair. That's a wrinkle. That's a bruise. That's . . . crap . . . what is that? Just let me get dressed alone, all right?

Speaking of getting dressed, Lily, my child who scoffs at J.Crew's Crewcuts and lusts over the Justice catalog, frequently greets me with equally colorful commentary on my clothes. She tells me my clothes don't match, my clothes make me look "flat," or the color of my sweater is "kinda ugly." She is the Joan Rivers of the house, and she is ruthless.

The patch of white hairs, the stubble on my legs, the heels in need of exfoliating . . . nothing goes unnoticed by my lovely children. At the end of the day, as I read the boys bedtime stories, Evan inevitably focuses on my face. "What's *that* dot?" he will ask, pointing to the tiniest pore or a birthmark or a chicken pox scar. One by one, he counts them like he's counting sheep, falling asleep to the comfort of my imperfections.

It's a miracle that any mother has the slightest bit of self-esteem left after the criticism our children and peers put us through on a daily basis. If men were treated like this, I'm quite sure that they would just crawl back into bed for the rest of their lives and mope about their feelings being hurt. But not us. We can take whatever the world throws at us and power on. Our skin isn't thick, it's impenetrable. Or getting there, at least.

And, may I just say, you're way too hard on yourself. We all think you're doing a great job.

# ★ The Seven Stages of ★
## Getting Dressed for a Rare Night Out

**1. SHOCK & DENIAL.** This is *not* my body. This is *NOT* my body. These are not my boobs, this is not my ass, these are not my thighs. No, no, no! This cannot be.

**2. PAIN & GUILT.** What have I been thinking eating like I'm still pregnant? I deserve this ass. I deserve this stomach. I deserve these thighs. I suck.

**3. ANGER.** What are you looking at? You've never seen a woman surrounded by the entire contents of her closet and three pints of ice cream? Go to hell. You're the one who caused me to look like this. You and your fucking sperm. You are the last person I want to go out with.

**4. DEPRESSION, REFLECTION, AND LONELINESS.** Why am I sitting here alone in my closet? It's because I look like this, isn't it? Nobody wants me.

**5. THE UPWARD TURN.** I don't have to look like this forever. I can start a diet RIGHT NOW. No carbs. No sugar. Gallons of water. MILF-dom, here I come!

**6. RECONSTRUCTION & WORKING THOUGH.** Okay, so maybe not *no* carbs. *Light* carbs. A *little* sugar. Iced tea. Vodka.

**7. ACCEPTANCE.** I'm never going to rock the skinny jeans or swimsuit again. Pass the Ben & Jerry's. And the muumuu. And the wine.

## Lie #12

# GOING FROM TWO TO THREE KIDS IS A BREEZE

$$| + | + | =$$

My number-one reason for not wanting to have a third baby is that I pee my pants pretty much every day since my second was born two years ago. At this rate, my kids will soon be more potty-trained than me.

—*Scary Mommy Confession* #117879

I was feeling pretty cocky back in February 2006. I'd successfully survived the first two years of motherhood with Lily and effortlessly brought a new baby into the house. The first time I had a baby I felt like the proverbial deer in the headlights, but this time I was an Experienced Mother, and my baby was clearly the child of an Experienced Mother. He slept through the night in his room immediately because I actually let him, and he was content almost twenty-four hours a day because I wasn't fussing with him constantly. With Lily, I waited almost a month before venturing past the front stoop, but when Ben was a baby, the three of us were out and about immediately. I didn't panic over silly things like stained Onesies and dirty car seats. I laughed at first-time mothers who used things like wipe warmers and bottle sanitizers and Diaper Genies. I relished being on the experienced side of the fence. I had this motherhood thing down.

My standing as Experienced Mother suffered a blow when I found out I was expecting another baby when Ben was only a year old. Sure, I could handle the two of them like a pro, but would three be as easy? I wasn't so sure. A neighbor and mother of four convinced me that I could handle it. Actually, she went even further: "Once you have two kids, you'll barely even notice another one," she confidently said. You'd think I'd learned my lesson about listening to people after that nurse's sage wisdom a few years before, but I hadn't. I ate up her every word.

Maybe I'd be like the Duggers, I thought, popping out a baby every year. If it was as effortless as it sounded, why not? I'd get to hold and enjoy sweet newborns and then move on to the next pregnancy while my older kids raised the younger ones. Didn't sound like such a bad gig.

And then Evan arrived. His birth would prove indicative of his entire existence. Unlike Ben, who came out clean and smiling, Evan was a bloody mess. Literally. Not only was he covered in baby goo, but a blood vessel in the umbilical cord popped as he made his way out and the entire room was sprayed in bright red blood. It was straight out of a bad horror movie and the perfect entrance for the baby who would change my world as I knew it.

The dynamic of going from two kids to three kids is kind of

like going from pulling up to Portofino, Italy, in a beautiful yacht in perfect, cloudless weather to finding yourself on the *Titanic* after its collision with the iceberg. You know the scene in the movie where the passengers are running for their lives as the boat tilts ninety degrees, and if they're not in a raft by that point, they're toast and they know it? That's what having three kids is like for me. On a good day.

In my defense, it's really a matter of physical limitations: A mother's body is clearly built for two kids. Two arms to wrap around their shoulders. Two hands to hold. Two ears to listen with. Two knees to bounce children on. Two hips to balance them on. Two cheeks to be kissed. It doesn't take a mathematician to see that something doesn't add up when you throw a third kid into the mix.

When you have two kids, sending your child to a friend's house for a sleepover makes you feel lonely. When you have three kids, it makes you feel like break-dancing.

When you have two kids, going out to dinner at a restaurant is a special treat. When you have three kids, the chances of one of them not living to see breakfast triples.

When you have two kids, finding a babysitter is a piece of cake. When you have three kids, you're lucky if your own parents will agree to watch them.

When you have two kids, you occasionally feel like a chauffeur. When you have three kids, you feel like a bus driver.

In all honesty, it's not always that bad. In general I love having three children, mostly because it increases the odds that I like at least one of my kids on any given day. But to claim that I'd barely notice the difference, as my neighbor suggested? That's

# ★ The Tragic Evolution of Motherhood ★

## YOU CHANGE A DIAPER . . .

*First baby:* Every hour, whether they need it or not.

*Second baby:* Every two to three hours, if necessary.

*Third baby:* Once it's sagging to their knees or strangers point out the smell.

## YOUR NEWBORN'S CLOTHES . . .

*First baby:* Are pre-washed, color coordinated, and folded into perfect little stacks in his or her dresser.

*Second baby:* You live out of the dryer and graciously accept stained hand-me-downs.

*Third baby:* Leaves the house in nothing but a diaper and rain boots.

## IF THE PACIFIER FALLS ON THE FLOOR, YOU . . .

*First baby:* Put it away until you can go home and sterilize it.

*Second baby:* Find a sink to rinse it in or water glass to dunk it in.

*Third baby:* Suck it clean yourself.

## THE BABY BOOK IS . . .

*First baby:* Completed daily with every minute detail of baby's day.

*Second baby:* Random baby pictures thrown into a shoe box.

*Third baby:* Didn't the hospital snap a picture for identification purposes?

### FIRST FOOD . . .

*First baby:* Pureed homegrown butternut squash.

*Second baby:* Gerber's organic baby food.

*Third baby:* A dog biscuit swiped from the dog when no one was looking.

### YOU HEAD TO THE PEDIATRICIAN . . .

*First baby:* At the very first sign of distress.

*Second baby:* When the baby's been acting fussy for a week.

*Third baby:* When you remember that you never made the well visit he was due for three months earlier.

### A DAY WITH BABY . . .

*First baby:* Mommy and Me classes, playgroups, baby gymnastics.

*Second baby:* A play group filled with your girlfriends and a glass of wine.

*Third baby:* The supermarket, the dry cleaner, and the liquor store.

## Lie #13

# THE PARENT
# IS IN CHARGE

Our home is run by a tyrant and we're all just his slaves.
He's four years old.

—*Scary Mommy Confession #254123*

One of the theoretical perks of parenthood is that you're always in charge. No matter whom you answer to at work, you are boss at home. Everyone under your roof answers to you, and you answer to no one. Right? Like I said, it's a *theoretical* perk. Kind of like how people say that owning and walking a dog keeps you healthy. Good concept in theory, but in reality you just end up stepping in shit most days.

Many parents would like you to believe that they are always in charge—that they lay down the law and their little ones fall into place like dominos. They are the ones with the education. They've read the parenting books. They have age and wisdom on their side.

I'm not one of those parents. Actually, I might be the one person in the house with the *least* amount of control over what happens.

It's apparent the moment you pull up outside of my home that I've completely surrendered. The lawn is littered with plastic balls and hula-hoops and bikes. It's like a nonstop scavenger hunt, with no prize at the finish. It wasn't always like this. I used to be militant about the kids putting away all of their junk when they were done playing. I wanted passersby to walk by my house and think *what a beautiful home,* but I fear the more common sentiment these days is *I didn't know there was an orphanage in this neighborhood.* The kids simply wore me down, and I honestly stopped caring. Jeff—bless his heart—still tries to keep the yard toy-free, but then again he also still thinks girls don't fart, so clearly he's not a realist.

Sadly, the inside of my house is worse. Long gone are the days when I could dictate the décor in my own home. Now couches are covered in mystery stains, the kitchen counter stools are dripping with jam from food fights over breakfast, and I don't think I've seen the playroom rug since we laid it down last year.

Before kids, Jeff and I used to save up our money to spend on decorating our house. Every few months, we'd stumble across something we loved: a whimsical painting to hang in the bedroom, a new flower vase for the foyer table, or maybe the perfect throw blanket for our couch. Carefully curating, purchase by purchase, we made our house a home. Boy, times have changed. The most recent piece of art I purchased was a shockingly insulting portrait of me drawn by my son. He drew me with not two, but three, chins, lopsided, triangular boobs, and a stomach the size of a small town. And I paid a dollar for it!

When did I relinquish control to my kids? When did *my* house become *their* house?

As if the physical state of my house weren't bad enough, a look at my calendar for any given weekend illustrates just how much power my kids have. I don't recall the last Sunday when each kid didn't have at least one birthday party to attend. God got to rest on Sunday. Why can't I? Add to that Ben's tennis lessons, Lily's sleepovers, and Evan's constant desire to play, and I'm counting the minutes until my shift as chauffeur is over once I drop them off at school on Monday.

Motherhood has also forced me to surrender control over my moods. It doesn't matter what side of the bed I wake up on; the only thing that matters is what side *they* wake up on. This is especially true of Ben. Of all of my children, Ben is the most reliably pleasant. Easy-natured and generally happy, Ben adds a desperately needed dose of serenity to our house. Usually. Every six days or so, my sweet Ben wakes up with a chip on his shoulder that knocks the wind out of me. Maybe it's because he is the middle child. Perhaps it's because his sister and brother demand so much attention that he can never get a word in. Whatever the reason, the kid turns into the devil at least once a week. Regardless of which kid is in a bad mood on any given day, it's totally contagious, and I end up spreading it to Jeff.

One need look no further than a family with young children out for dinner to see just who wears the pants. Sometimes the bargaining is so intense, I feel like I am at a flea market rather than a restaurant. If you eat five bites of chicken, then you can have french fries, I tell them. Drink your milk and then you can have some lemonade. If you sit still for fifteen minutes you can have dessert. It's awful, but it's a small price to pay to have someone else cook dinner and wash the dishes. I've even resorted to smuggling PB&J sandwiches into restaurants just to get out of the house and then feigning surprise when the kids tell the waiter they're just not hungry.

I've lost count of all the things that were once mine that I am now forced to share with my kids. Lily frequently uses my lip gloss, leaving it uncovered and crusty. Ben insists on hiding all of our television remote controls so his brother and sister can't change the channel when he is watching a show, which might be cute if he ever remembered where he put them. And Evan thinks my new iPhone actually belongs to him.

I can't really pinpoint the exact moment when I relinquished control. Honestly, I don't know if I ever had it—first kids take over your body, then they take over your life. And I suppose I'm okay with that.

After all, I still get to control my husband.

# ★ Murphy's Laws of Family Vacations ★

• The night before departure, your child will come down with a cough, cold, or broken limb.

• They will have to pee—so bad—three seconds after takeoff, despite having gone to the bathroom directly before boarding.

• They will refuse to eat the very same six-dollar macaroni and cheese that they inhale at home, when presented with it at an overpriced restaurant.

• You will forget to pack at least one of the following: enough diapers or Pull-Ups, your cell phone charger, toothpaste other than SpongeBob SquarePants gel, or that most special teddy bear.

• You will be completely unable to capture a smiling picture of your children in the adorable outfits you packed for that very purpose. Ever.

• They will be up at the crack of dawn, ready for immediate entertainment, whereas they sleep soundly until seven at home.

• You will spend an hour packing everything you can think of for the beach, only to be told twenty minutes in that your child is bored and wants to leave.

• They will miss the toys they never play with at home and the rooms they never want to spend time in. Upon returning home, they won't have any interest in either.

• The souvenirs you purchase will break or be lost before you even make it back home.

• You will come back from vacation in dire need of a vacation. Without the kids.

# MOTHER'S DAY IS ALL ABOUT YOU

For Mother's Day, I will trim my pubes. And then I'll pleasure myself while fantasizing about child-free days, endless bottles of wine, and the time when my husband was actually sexy.

—*Scary Mommy Confession #99281*

Once a year in May, there is that glorious day celebrating all things motherhood. The day we finally get to sit back and not lift a finger and bathe in the accolades our loved ones shower upon us. The day when we get a year's worth of recognition for all the sacrifices we've made and appreciation for all the little things we do. When we get to relax and breathe in and not spend the day cleaning or overseeing or decision-making . . . or, not.

It turns out Mother's Day is the episiotomy of motherhood: it's supposed to be for your benefit but you're the one making all the sacrifices.

Of all the lies of motherhood, I think this one might be the cruelest. I feel so sorry for new mothers, who tend to look forward to their first Mother's Day with their newborns with the same anticipation they had for the actual birth of their children. I've been there, and my own visions of photo ops, adorable clothing, and an outpouring of appreciation were quickly squashed with the harsh reality that there are no days off in motherhood. Especially in year one.

Somehow, instead of a day spent lounging on the couch with our hands down our pants like our male counterparts on *their* day, Mother's Day has turned into yet another day where we are expected to work our asses off.

In the best of Hallmark worlds, ours is a day filled with brunches, bouquets of flowers, and homemade gifts. Super, but who is going to make the actual reservation for brunch? And who is going to spend the morning struggling to gets the kids dressed in clean clothes that fit? And who is going to be stuck changing the water in that flower vase for the next several days? We are, that's who! Mother's Day gives new meaning to the word *motherfucker*. We're the ones getting fucked.

How about breakfast in bed? Such a sweet notion in theory, but in actuality, it's the worst gift a child can give. Let's let the kids loose in the kitchen while we're still asleep, oblivious that the house is about to burn down! Perfect! One year, Lily presented me with a plate of toast and some sliced berries. The cinnamon-sugar toast was edible, I was delighted to discover, and I gratefully ate it. Could have been so much worse, I thought, as I debated turning over some cooking responsibilities to my little chef.

Until I went down to the kitchen and discovered what looked like World War III. There was jam plastered on the refrigerator and cinnamon sprinkled across the floor. There were cracked eggs on the counter, the yolks oozing down the granite. The dog was frantically eating the rest of the loaf of bread that Lily left out on the table, and God knows what else that pup ingested. (As a bonus, I found out later that night. And again at 3 a.m.!) Every single cabinet was open, and the sink was overflowing with every utensil in the house—all for a piece of toast and a few strawberries. There's a reason brunch is really only meant to be eaten out, I quickly learned.

My husband and I have an argument every single year when he asks what I want to do for Mother's Day. I want to be left alone, I say, every single year. But it's *Mother's Day,* he argues. Don't you want to spend it with your children?

No, I don't, thank you very much, I answer. I spend every day with my children, and I am lucky to do so. But, shouldn't a holiday be treated differently than just another ordinary day? Yes, it should. So, every Mother's Day, all I ask is one simple thing: to be left the hell alone.

I tried this approach last year. I slept late and played dead when I heard the kids calling for me. I took a shower by myself and without an audience, and I might have even had an uninterrupted bowel movement. I didn't do any laundry, and I cooked nothing. Jeff took the kids out for several hours, and I had the house all to myself. It was wonderful—for about an hour. That's how long it took before I started feeling like something was off, like I had lost a limb or something. Before I knew it, I was missing my kids. I longed for their hugs and slobbery kisses, and I

# ★ You Thought You Were Special? ★

Turns out having an annual holiday celebrated in your honor is hardly that big of a deal. Everybody and their mother has their own damn holiday.

**JANUARY 10** is Houseplant Appreciation Day

**JANUARY 14** is Dress Up Your Pet Day

**JANUARY 15** is National Hat Day

**JANUARY 20** is Penguin Awareness Day

**JANUARY 28** is National Kazoo Day

**FEBRUARY 5** is National Weatherman's Day

**FEBRUARY 19** is National Chocolate Mint Day

**FEBRUARY 23** is International Dog Biscuit Appreciation Day

**FEBRUARY 26** is National Pistachio Day

**MARCH 1** is National Pig Day

**MARCH 6** is National Frozen Food Day

**MARCH 10** is Middle Name Pride Day

**MARCH 14** is Learn About Butterflies Day

**MARCH 20** is Extraterrestrial Abductions Day

**MARCH 24** is National Chocolate-Covered Raisin Day

**APRIL 2** is National Peanut Butter and Jelly Day

**APRIL 4** is Hug a Newsman Day

**APRIL 16** is National Stress Awareness Day

**APRIL 18** is International Juggler's Day

**APRIL 26** is Hug an Australian Day

**APRIL 30** is Hairstyle Appreciation Day

**MAY 4** is National Candied Orange Peel Day

**MAY 6** is National Tourist Appreciation Day

**MAY 16** is Love a Tree Day

**JUNE 6** is National Yo-Yo Day

**JUNE 19** is World Sauntering Day

**JUNE 28** is Insurance Awareness Day

**JULY 7** is National Strawberry Sundae Day

**JULY 13** is Barbershop Music Appreciation Day

**JULY 18** is National Caviar Day

**AUGUST 6** is Wiggle Your Toes Day

**AUGUST 18** is Bad Poetry Day

**AUGUST 31** is National Trail Mix Day

**SEPTEMBER 2** is National Beheading Day

**SEPTEMBER 5** is Cheese Pizza Day

**SEPTEMBER 22** is Elephant Appreciation Day

**OCTOBER 2** is National Custodial Worker Day

**OCTOBER 8** is American Touch Tag Day

**OCTOBER 24** is National Bologna Day

**NOVEMBER 2** is Deviled Egg Day

**NOVEMBER 13** is National Indian Pudding Day

**NOVEMBER 29** Square Dance Day

**DECEMBER 1** is Eat a Red Apple Day

**DECEMBER 18** is National Roast Suckling Pig Day

**DECEMBER 27** is National Fruitcake Day

*Lie #15*

# IT GETS EASIER

I went grocery shopping by myself for the first time in six years. I spent an embarrassingly long time in the detergent aisle opening each one and inhaling the heavenly scent of peace and quiet.

—*Scary Mommy Confession #228532*

When you see a new mother attempting to maneuver her oversized stroller through a too-small door, while her baby is screaming bloody murder and she is carrying three bags of groceries and looking like she is about to lose her mind, you will no doubt be tempted to rush to her aid, hold the door, and tell her gently that things will get easier.

STOP. Don't you dare.

I mean, hold the door for her and help with the bags, of course, even offer to buy her a cup of coffee, if you're so inclined. But please, whatever you do, do *not* go telling her that things will get easier. They won't.

Go ahead and tell her that she won't always be walking through life in a complete haze or sterilizing baby bottles for the rest of her life. Tell her that there will be a day in the not so distant future when she won't be covered in spit-up, or still futilely trying to master the correct way to swaddle. She won't always be unshowered and mentally exhausted and ready to cry at any and every moment in time. But parenting *doesn't* get any easier, and you know it and I know it.

You know that sinking feeling when you start a new job and on the first day you have that moment when you start to wonder what the hell you've gotten yourself into, and if it's not too late to get out? That's kind of how I felt my first few weeks on the job of motherhood. I wasn't sleeping on a schedule that I dictated, my days revolved around feeding and changing and burping, and I still felt like a live science experiment gone bad. *This* was the light at the end of my nine-month-long tunnel? I wanted my money back, thank you very much. My husband would come home from work and I'd be torn between wanting to hear about his day, for the first adult interaction I'd had in hours, and resenting that he got to have adult interaction all day. I was an absolute mess.

My experience with my subsequent children's early days was an entirely different story. After reacquainting myself with adult interaction, I'd decided it wasn't all it was cracked up to be. Dealing with school parents and playdates with painfully awkward conversation, and getting my decisions critiqued by people I barely knew? Being home alone with a sweet baby during rounds two and three didn't seem so bad at all. What had my problem been, exactly?

Once my first baby grew up a bit, I also gained an appreciation for just how easy those early days truly are. They were undoubtedly draining, but there was nothing *challenging* about them. In most cases, a newborn can be soothed with one of three things: a clean diaper, a bottle, or a boob. Boring? Sure. But hard? No. Not even a little. Rocking a baby the second and third time around seemed like a pleasure cruise compared to the temper tantrums and potty training I was dealing with from my older child.

Instead of staring too long at the hot barista who serves me coffee or the UPS man who used to turn me on, I stare longingly at infants, frequently causing their mothers to uncomfortably relocate far outside my gaze. Now, as I'm helping with homework I have no idea how to do or engaging in an epic battle over "all my friends wear bikinis and have cell phones, why can't I," I fantasize about stealing a baby, inventing a time-freeze machine, and never looking back.

So, I'm sorry, new moms. As much as you are suffering, it's only going to get worse. I am quite certain that no matter how tired and overwhelmed you are, someday you will look back at this fleeting period in your life and laugh at your stressed-out and oblivious self. Welcome to the club.

# ★ Good News, Bad News ★

**THE GOOD NEWS:** You will not be doing three loads of Onesies a day forever.

**THE BAD NEWS:** The clothes only get bigger. Sure, you won't need to wash out baby puke and clean up after explosive diarrhea that seeped out of the diaper, but the laundry only gets worse. Kids want to change sixteen times a day. And they trip on grass. And play sports. And eat like pigs. The laundry doesn't stop, and the clothes only get a hell of a lot less cute to fold.

**THE GOOD NEWS:** You won't always be schlepping around an infant carrier.

**THE BAD NEWS:** You'll never again be able to seamlessly move a sleeping child into the house.

**THE GOOD NEWS:** Your baby won't always be a blob and will actually smile at you soon!

**THE BAD NEWS:** Shortly after that first smile, they also will scowl and frown and pout.

**THE GOOD NEWS:** You won't be breastfeeding forever.

**THE BAD NEWS:** You'll go right back to that pre-pregnancy cup size.

**THE GOOD NEWS:** You won't be reading stupid board books forever.
**THE BAD NEWS:** You'll need to help out with homework that you have no idea how to do.

**THE GOOD NEWS:** Your child will one day be able to articulate his or her needs.
**THE BAD NEWS:** Your child will one day articulate *every single need*.

**THE GOOD NEWS:** You will soon hear the word *mommy* and it will be the most wonderful sound in the universe.
**THE BAD NEWS:** Soon after, you will hear the word *MOMMY!!* five hundred times in a row and it will be the most irritating word you have ever heard in your life.

**THE GOOD NEWS:** Your child will eventually sleep through the night.
**THE BAD NEWS:** *You* will never get a full night's sleep again. You'll be awoken by bad dreams and wet beds, and one day inevitably stay awake waiting for your teenager to waltz through the door three seconds before curfew. Sleep as you once knew it is over. Forever.

## *Lie* #16
# PETS MAKE CHILDREN MORE RESPONSIBLE

I hate rodents more than anything, but got a gerbil for my daughter because it was all she wanted for her birthday. Gerbil got sick and guess who feeds the damn rat her meds through a little baby syringe and sings lullabies the whole time? My daughter? HA.

—*Scary Mommy Confession* #258866

Our beloved twelve-year-old golden retriever, Penelope, passed away last spring. Her health had been declining for several months, and one day she woke up simply unable to stand. We brought her to the vet and heard the devastating news we had known was coming for a while: the time had come to put her out of her pain. And, so, we did. We said our tearful goodbyes as she peacefully took her last breaths. We kissed her head and patted her tummy as we lay with her, thanking her for being such a wonderful pet to us.

For weeks, Jeff and I walked around in a complete daze. We had brought Penelope home a few weeks after we were married and could barely remember a life together that didn't include her. I would sporadically cry, countless times throughout the day, and unexpectedly finding a tuft of her hair reduced me to a sobbing mess for hours one afternoon. The void she left in the house was palpable, so much more so than I ever could have imagined. But the kids seemed relatively unfazed. Sure, they were sad, but life went on. They bickered and played and antagonized and didn't seem interested in wallowing the way I did.

Lying in bed one night, I asked Jeff why he thought the kids weren't more of a mess. Didn't they miss her red tail wagging? Greeting her upon entering the house? Feeding her their un-wanted chicken fingers? Apparently Jeff wasn't all that surprised. They're kids, was his simple answer. They bounce back quickly; I doubt they'll even remember her when they're grown.

*WHAT??! OF COURSE* they will, I cried. They loved her!! They grew up with her! They rode her like a horse! They chased her around the house! They fed her their food! They played in the snow! Of course, they'll remember those things . . . Forever! Won't they?!!?

I'm not sure they will, he insisted. They're so little now—do you remember much from when you were five or six? Pe-nelope was *our* dog, before kids. They knew her for a while, but she wasn't our *family* dog. She wasn't the dog who slept in their rooms and whom they could actually walk themselves. She wasn't the dog they really helped with. By the time they were born, she was old. They missed out on all of that.

And then he uttered the words that started it all: they really do need a dog of their own.

For the next several months, Jeff began a campaign that could rival any billion-dollar run for office. You see, as much as I adored my Penny, I had also become quite accustomed to the perks of *not* having a dog. The fact that I didn't have to vacuum every day. That I hadn't picked up a lint brush in weeks. Not walking a dog in the rain. Not scheduling my day around being home for walks and remembering to dole out flea medication. Turns out, there are lots of nice things about that palpable void in the house.

But Jeff didn't agree. To him, having our children grow up without a dog (like the two of us did, I might note) was unfathomable. His list of reasons included unconditional love, added exercise, and, of course, the teaching of responsibility. The most loving and responsible adults had dogs when they were children, he pulled out of his ass like he had spent years hypothesizing it. We went around in circles for weeks, me gleefully wearing all the black I could without it being covered in dog hair, and him pointing out any time one of the children did something the least bit irresponsible. Having a pet of their own will make the kids more responsible, he insisted. As he does about most things, he wore me down, and in the fall, we brought home a new puppy.

A sweet golden retriever, just like Penelope, Maisy will be the dog who is prominently featured in childhood pictures, greets the kids after school, and hopefully, will even be around to see Lily off to college. She will be our family dog, and they will infinitely benefit from having her. And most of all, this dog will be the one to teach my children about responsibility and whip them the hell into shape.

Or, not.

Back when Jeff was busy convincing me that getting a pet would make our kids more responsible (what a fucking liar), I made a list in my head of all the ways this prediction would come true.

They'll be more responsible about putting their stuff away, I told myself. Now, five months into the Maisy Era, I can say that's not exactly how it has turned out. The minute my kids come in the door, they kick (Kick! They don't even have the courtesy to toss) their shoes on the floor. Next come their coats, and their backpacks follow. I have warned them a million times that Maisy will chew their shoes and their homework. And, of course, they haven't heeded my warning. Lily's new Uggs are discolored due to excess dog saliva. And on more than one occasion, Maisy has *literally* eaten Ben's homework.

Well, I told myself, at least having a dog will help make the kids more responsible when it comes to being gentle with pets. Yeah, not really sure how that is working out, either. I am totally convinced that Maisy thinks Evan is a puppy, and she plays with him as if he were her littermate. And he loves it. He puts his face in her mouth, and her face in his mouth. He rides her like a pony, and I once saw him trying to put her in a chokehold. While I had hoped that having a puppy would make my kids veterinarian-like in their care and concern for animals, I worry that they're actually becoming more like Michael Vick instead.

I had high hopes for all the other ways in which bringing Maisy into the family would make my kids more responsible.

Additional dog duties will help them balance their daily tasks, I thought. They'll be more careful not to drop food on the floor or leave it out on the counters. And guess what? Some mornings the dog eats three times, as all of the kids feed her without checking if the other already did, and on other mornings she isn't fed at all. And as far as kitchen cleanliness goes, my kitchen has never been filthier. Rather than complain to me about finishing their food, now the kids just slyly throw everything they don't want onto the floor, assuming Maisy will finish it.

As you might guess, poor Maisy has diarrhea. All the time.

In the long list of times I should have known better than to listen to my husband, this is near the top. I'm already plotting my revenge, though. I'm trying to convince him that getting a vasectomy will make me want to have sex with him more.

Fool!

# ★ Babies Versus Puppies ★

When babies have a tummy ache, they contain the mess to their diapers. When puppies have a tummy ache, they insist on taking it out on your lightest-colored rug.

When babies teethe, they simply fuss. When puppies teethe, they ruin your favorite pairs of shoes.

When babies need a bath, they can be gently washed down in a baby bath tub and dried off with a small towel. When puppies need a bath, the bathroom looks like it's survived a typhoon and every towel in your house is sopping wet.

When babies are sick, pediatrician's visits are paid for by insurance. When puppies are sick, you can kiss that vacation you were saving for goodbye.

When babies come in from the rain, they may need a change of clothing. When puppies come in from the rain, you want to move to a new house.

When a new baby enters your life, people rush to your aid and can't wait to help out in any way they can. When a new puppy enters your life, people think you're insane.

*Lie #17*

# A HOUSE WITHOUT CHILDREN
# IS AN EMPTY ONE

My kids think I'm kidding when I say I can't wait to sign myself into a retirement community where they will need an appointment to visit me.

—*Scary Mommy Confession #111354*

We picked Maisy out from a farm about two hours away. You know, to begin our quest to see just how much neediness Mommy can take before she goes bat-shit crazy.

After a rough drive that included Evan vomiting all over himself, we pulled up to a beautiful farm of rolling hills and mature trees. Horses meandered calmly in the fields. Birds chirped happily and melodically. There was a calmness about the place that almost made me forget about the stench of Evan's soiled clothes. In the distance, I could see two large golden retrievers watching us approach. The puppies' parents! I was excited to see them, but as I got closer and got a better view, my excitement turned to horror.

The sire looked fantastic. Smiling widely and wagging his tail profusely, he was robust and healthy looking. His coat was wavy and soft, and his eyes sparkled with joy and excitement. He looked proud of his puppies and maybe even of his virility.

And then there was the mother. This bitch was a mess. She looked like she hadn't slept in days, and her coat was knotted and gnarly. I'm pretty sure I saw food dangling from her ear. But that wasn't the worst of it. As she got up and made her way over to me, I saw her battle scars: dangling from her underbelly were seven—SEVEN—saggy, sore, blistered nipples. They were like testicles, only uglier. That poor, poor dog, I thought to myself, as we came face-to-face.

And just as I was starting to feel guilty about taking one of her beloved puppies away from her for the rest of her life, we shared a moment that I'll never forget. As we locked eyes, mother to mother, she gave me a look of sheer relief. "Thank fucking God," her eyes said. "Better you than me. Better you than me."

I swear, if that dog could have packed that puppy's suitcase and put it in my trunk herself she would have had us on our way home without a minute to spare. She was Done with a capital D. We would leave the farm that day with our new puppy in tow, and her mother would get her life and her body back. There wasn't even a hint of sorrow. I'd call it jubilation.

And I can't say I didn't recognize the feeling.

I sent each of my kids to full-day preschool when they turned two. With Lily, it felt like a necessity. Ben was born the same month that she turned two, and I simply needed the help during the day. The same thing happened with Ben when Evan was born just twenty-one months later. Once again, I had a newborn in the house and needed time to devote to my new baby. But then Evan turned two, and I had no excuse. For a few weeks I even thought about having another baby just so I could rationalize packing Evan off to preschool. But that would have killed me, and then what good would I be to my kids? So I sent him off, too, and waited for the flood of guilt and sorrow to hit. And I waited. And waited. And waited.

It never came. Suddenly, for the first time in five years, I wasn't stuck home every day with a baby. I could take long showers and do my hair. I could leisurely read *People* magazine at lunch, rather than in the checkout aisle. I didn't have to change my clothes twice a day, and I could spend hours at HomeGoods looking at décor I didn't need. It was heavenly. Perhaps it was because I knew I would see my kids at the end of each day, but I never missed them for a minute while they were at preschool. I savored picking them up and seeing their joyful faces as they ran toward me with arms outstretched, but I also relished the six hours of me time I had each day.

Childless vacations were hard to swallow at first. Jeff would frequently suggest that we get away, but I just couldn't get comfortable with the idea of leaving my kids behind. What kind of mother would leave her kids home while she indulged in fun and relaxation? Me, it turns out.

We started out small. A weekend away, only a few hours' drive from home. Then we worked our way up to four days and a plane ride. Before we knew it, we were on a full-blown adult vacation. Sure, I thought about my kids and looked forward to seeing them when I returned home. But miss them? Not as much as I expected to.

When Lily became old enough for sleepovers, things only got better. One less kid whom I have to nag to brush her teeth. One less story to read. One less kid to force to take a bath or shower. One less mouth to feed in the morning. At first, Jeff and I missed her when she would sleep out. The house seemed too quiet and didn't feel totally right. But we got over that pretty quickly. It wasn't long before we started to appreciate making our kid someone else's problem for a night. Now I keep a duffle bag of Lily's clothes and toiletries in the car, just in case an invitation for a sleepover comes our way. What can I say? We believe in the Boy Scout motto: Be prepared.

Now we're starting to think about sleepaway camp. It's something I never thought I would even entertain, but now that I've been a mother for nine years, I've seen the light. My turning point was this past summer, when one of Lily's friends went to overnight camp for six weeks. At first, I couldn't believe her parents would send their baby away for that long. How would they sleep at night not knowing what their little girl had for dinner? And what if she got sick and landed in the infirmary? How could a registered nurse possibly give her the necessary care?

But then I saw the parents out for dinner one night when Jeff and I ended up at the same restaurant. While we scarfed down our food to hurry up and get home to the babysitter before we were out eighty bucks, they seemed to take their time. While they drank wine and nibbled on appetizers, we paid the bill before the food even came to the table. We stopped by their table to say hello on our way out, and the first thing I noticed was how well rested they looked. Tanned and toned, it appeared that they were enjoying their summer. They regaled us with stories about the letters they received from their daughter each day, recounting the fun she was having and the friendships she was forging. They told us about the two-week trip they were about to take and about all the movies they had seen so far that summer. While I thought about flipping their table over Real Housewives–style then and there, I restrained myself, and Jeff and I sheepishly shuffled out of the restaurant and to our car like two middle schoolers who just lost their lunch money to the school bully.

I spent the rest of the night researching summer camps online, and I have every intention of sending my kids to overnight camp when they're ready. Or when I'm ready, whichever comes first.

I realize that, because my kids are still young, I'll likely eat these words when they leave my home for college and start their own lives, somewhere else. I've seen my own parents struggle with an empty nest and I know I'll someday long for the madness that is my life right now. But for now I'm just trying to get to tomorrow.

And hoping it's a sleepover weekend.

# ★ Rules for Playdates ★

## (TO BE REPEATED BY YOUR CHILD'S PLAYMATE)

**1.** I will arrive on time. I know from experience how annoying it is to be told a playdate is starting at one time and then not having it begin until an hour later.

**2.** I will kiss my mother goodbye. I know that I'll see her soon, and you both have better things to do than engage in pointless small talk.

**3.** I will not ask you to endlessly throw balls/do art projects/referee sports/run around after me. I recognize that my sole job is to entertain your child.

**4.** I won't want to watch TV. TV is the babysitter you use when your kid is alone and you are desperate. I won't ask you to waste it on me.

**5.** I will not ask for another snack, three seconds after finishing my first. Actually, I'm not hungry at all, thank you very much.

**6.** I will clean up the mess I made. Every last LEGO.

**7.** I'll respect that you have your rules and I have mine. Just because I play video games all day/drink soda/attempt to fly off of furniture at home, doesn't mean I expect to at your home.

**8.** I will include your other children. Pesky little sibling? No way! Just another kid I get to play with.

**9.** I won't leave remnants of number one around your toilet. And I most definitely won't leave remnants of number two.

**10.** Next time, I'll have the playdate at my house.

*Lie #18*

# YOU'LL LOOK FORWARD TO
# YOUR KIDS' INDEPENDENCE

I remember thinking how cute it was when my child
learned how to take off her own diaper. Until I came in
one morning and saw her finger painting and it wasn't
paint she was painting with.

—*Scary Mommy Confession #254518*

I remember my children's first steps like they were yesterday. That magical moment when they no longer needed to hold on to my fingers to make it across the room was everything I hoped it would be and more. It was so exciting and gratifying and my heart swelled with pride all three times. It's the kind of moment that makes this whole mommy thing worth it.

That was then. This is now.

Years later, I can't help but wonder what the hell I was so excited about. My kids figuring out that they were their own people, rather than simply extensions of me? Their growing

---

*Lie #18*

# YOU'LL LOOK FORWARD TO YOUR KIDS' INDEPENDENCE

I remember thinking how cute it was when my child learned how to take off her own diaper. Until I came in one morning and saw her finger painting and it wasn't paint she was painting with.

—*Scary Mommy Confession #254518*

I remember my children's first steps like they were yesterday. That magical moment when they no longer needed to hold on to my fingers to make it across the room was everything I hoped it would be and more. It was so exciting and gratifying and my heart swelled with pride all three times. It's the kind of moment that makes this whole mommy thing worth it.

That was then. This is now.

Years later, I can't help but wonder what the hell I was so excited about. My kids figuring out that they were their own people, rather than simply extensions of me? Their growing awareness that I don't have all the answers? Turns out, our children's independence is completely overrated.

Once my children walked, they never stopped moving. Gone were the days when I could leave them and go to the bathroom—gasp—alone, or take a phone call in the other room while they contentedly played on the floor. Suddenly I was held hostage in my own house, stuck in a never-ending game of cat-and-mouse. But only one of us was having fun.

I naïvely counted down the days until my kids could dress themselves so I wouldn't have to leave three piles of clothes on the banister every morning. Well, the day has arrived and it's bad. Bad with glitter and ruffles and mismatched patterns. I mean, I know you're supposed to foster creativity in your children, but what if your child has indisputably horrific taste? Are you supposed to encourage *that*? These days, I have to hide the Justice catalog from Lily as I longingly look at siblings dressed in matching pajamas over at L.L.Bean.

I long for the Halloweens that came before my children could make decisions for themselves aka the good old days when I could dress them up as I pleased. A princess and a frog prince! Cowboy and cowgirl! Wild animals and me as the zookeeper! A trio of superheroes! Pictures are proudly displayed throughout the house, and holiday cards with my agreeable children still adorn friends' refrigerators years later.

That was then. This is now.

For Halloween 2012 Ben was a Star Wars character, Evan was Wolverine, and Lily was dressed as a zombie prom queen. I died a little that day. There was no theme even I could concoct with those three costumes, and I haven't even bothered to print out pictures, never mind frame them.

Once upon a time, my children were friends with the kids I hand-selected for them. I was very discerning. The kid who coughed all the time? Not for us. Little girl who lived almost an hour a way? No thanks. The twin boys in Ben's preschool class? Twin boys; need I say more? These days my kids tell me who they want to have over after school, and I have no say. The only sliver of control I maintain is the occasional fib about so-and-so being unavailable. But that only lasts so long, and eventually I am forced to entertain the kids who have recovered from the fake illnesses I've assigned to them.

As parents, we spend all of our time preparing our children for the world so they may live independently. After all, that's the name of the parenting game. But I can't help but wonder what the rush is. Why not extend their dependency as long as possible? Listen, I want them out of my house as soon as they're eighteen, like most parents do. I just want to make all of their decisions for them until then.

# ★ 25 Reasons NOT to Have a(nother) Baby ★

**1.** Morning sickness that has you throwing up in the kitchen sink because you just can't make it to the bathroom in time.

**2.** Stretch marks on top of stretch marks on top of stretch marks.

**3.** Not being able to wear your wedding ring because your fingers have morphed into sausages.

**4.** Sex with a fetus in the middle.

**5.** Cankles.

**6.** Not having your period, but having to still wear a pad.

**7.** The entire ninth month of pregnancy.

**8.** Changing crib sheets.

**9.** Taking that first shit after delivery.

**10.** The dried out, ready-to-fall-off umbilical cord.

**11.** The aerobic workout that is installing an infant car seat.

**12.** Running out of wipes at the worst possible moment in time.

**13.** Being on the receiving end of endless and unwanted advice on everything involving your baby.

**14.** Trying on your pre-baby jeans for the first time.

**15.** Realizing that the baby weight is *not* going to melt off.

**16.** Living in fear that you will wake that baby who took, OMG seriously, an hour and a half to put to sleep.

**17.** Cutting teeny, tiny, paper-thin fingernails.

**18.** Obsessively checking to make sure the baby is breathing when he or she is finally soundly asleep.

**19.** Rectally taking temperatures.

**20.** Projectile vomit.

**21.** Not being able to soothe a screaming baby in a backward-facing seat because you are concentrating on not wrapping your car around a tree, but at that moment it sounds like a fine way to put you out of your misery.

**22.** Searching in the middle of the night for a lost pacifier like it was a million-dollar lottery ticket.

**23.** Not being able to turn your head because you fall asleep night after night in the rocking chair.

**24.** Maneuvering a stroller around a store not built for strollers.

**25.** The fact that babies turn into . . . kids.

# ★ 25 Reasons TO Have a(nother) Baby ★

1. Not having a period for nine months.

2. Not having to suck in your gut.

3. The fun of being able to say "I'm not expecting" when asked how far along you are.

4. Not worrying about birth control.

5. Hearing the heartbeat for the first time.

6. Parking in "Expectant Mother" parking spaces.

7. The fact that nobody picks a fight with the pregnant woman.

8. Having your husband cater to your every whim.

9. The first shower after delivery.

10. The forty-eight-hour hospital stay.

11. Scouring Pinterest for the perfect way to announce the baby.

12. Introducing them to their new big sister or brother.

13. People bring you meals! And help you with laundry! And want to make your life easier!

14. That first precious Halloween costume.

15. Teeny, tiny baby toes.

**16.** The smell of their clean heads.

**17.** Catching adorable first moments and showing them off mercilessly.

**18.** The first smile.

**19.** The first giggle.

**20.** The epidural.

**21.** Precious little shoes that never get dirty.

**22.** Catching up on old episodes of *Dawson's Creek* and *Melrose Place*.

**23.** Having people ask to hold the baby verses having them run away from your kids.

**24.** Having an excuse to be unshowered.

**25.** Everything.

I did whatever I wanted, like take three-hour lunch breaks. I'd slip out of my office at about eleven and head to the outlet mall about thirty minutes away. Then I'd hit the gym, where I would use the steam room for a good twenty minutes after exercising. If it was a slow day at the office, I'd also stop at the brand-new Harris Teeter grocery store near my office and get our weekly food shopping out of the way. How perfect that we had a kitchen at the office where I could refrigerate my groceries!

My next job was as the design manager at one of my favorite stores. This was the first time that I actually enjoyed my work and felt a sense of fulfillment at the end of each day. Building an amazing window display that stopped patrons in their tracks was very rewarding. I used to love to bring Jeff into the store on the weekends and show him all the vignettes I had created. I didn't even mind the fact that the job required me to be in by 6 a.m. Monday through Friday. What I did mind, though, were the frequent visits from the district manager who would come in to the store and rearrange everything I had worked so hard on. I also hated it when I had to participate on pesky phone calls on P&L. Sure, I was in management, but I guess it never occurred to me that store performance had anything to do with—or any impact on—my design plans. Details, details.

When I got pregnant, I felt like I was the luckiest bitch in town. We moved out of the city and into a more affordable home, so that Jeff's single salary could support our growing family. I had no second thoughts about leaving the workforce. That's an understatement, actually. I think if I were even the slightest bit athletic I would have done cartwheels up and down our street. While I had moments of enjoyment and pride at my previous jobs, I never felt totally fulfilled. I never felt like I was following my calling.

After the chaos of having a newborn died down, I attacked my new job as a SAHM with vigor: Mommy and Me classes as often as possible; lunch dates with other moms and their babies; enough tummy time to make any pediatrician proud; three-course home-cooked meals for my husband. I quickly got into the rhythm of my new life, and I patiently waited for the over-whelming feeling of fulfillment to hit me.

And I kept waiting for the fulfillment. And waiting. And waiting.

If I had a dollar for every time someone told me that stay-ing home with my kids would be the most fulfilling job I'd ever have, I'd hire a really good hit man to kill all of those fucking liars.

And it wasn't just people I knew—even people I loved and trusted—feeding me this load of crap. Every women's magazine I read would have some article in it about the joys of stay-at-home-motherhood. Television shows at that time portrayed moms who stayed home with their kids as heroic, noble, and perky. Researchers and therapists would pontificate on morning shows about what a sense of accomplishment SAHMs experi-ence on a daily basis.

I have always loved being home with my children. It's pre-cious time for which I am enormously grateful and that I wouldn't trade for the world. But fulfilling? Not always. Not usually. It was especially tough at first, as I got used to all of the time at home. And I took it out on Jeff, who I'd pick a fight with nearly every night when he came home from work.

How was your day? What did you do, he would innocently ask.

*What did I do? WHAT DID I DO? I took care of your daughter. I read to her and bathed her and dressed her and cleaned up after her and ran around after her keeping her alive all day long. THAT'S WHAT I DID. How dare you insinuate that I sat on my ass all day doing nothing. You think I was eating bonbons and watching soaps? Why don't YOU try staying home?*

"Um . . . okay," he'd respond sheepishly. "What's for dinner?"

*What's for dinner? DINNER? What, I'm your personal chef, too? Seriously? I had a bowl of cereal for dinner. It was delicious.*

I'm actually pretty surprised he bothered coming back at all those first few months. If I'd been in his shoes, the Ramada Inn off the highway exit near us would have been home.

Considering how much I always despised working, my rough transition to stay-at-homedom confused even me. I didn't like answering to a boss or having to wear heels or fill out my hours or be held accountable when I inevitably fucked up. But once I gave up work, I missed many of the things I once resented. A long commute in the car translated to precious alone time. Water cooler conversation meant the adult interaction I craved. Even dressing up in stockings and a skirt sounded appealing after being covered in mystery slime all day.

"So, if you're so miserable, get a job," Jeff would say.

*And have someone else raise my baby??? Am I not doing it well? Nobody can love her like I do. I can't miss her first steps! And first smiles! What—she's going to say Mommy to someone else? I don't think so, JEFF. I wouldn't trade being home for anything in the world. OBVIOUSLY. You don't understand me at all!!!*

Of course he didn't understand me. *I* didn't understand me. I had exactly what I wanted and suddenly I wanted what I had always hated.

Then I got pregnant with Ben when Lily was just fifteen months, and before I knew it Evan came and I was a SAHM to three kids under the age of four. I found myself desperate for something more. My blog was born out of my need to find something to fulfill me outside of being a mommy. I remember the day I decided to start Scary Mommy. Lily and Ben were in preschool and Evan was napping. I decided to lie down on the couch and catch a quick nap myself while I could. As I lay there, thoughts were racing through my head, preventing me from falling asleep. Why is Caillou bald, I wondered. Does he have a disease? Do his parents shave his head? And what about Max and Ruby? Do they have parents? Is the trauma surrounding their death the reason that poor Max never speaks?

These thoughts were the last straw. I was determined to go out and find my fulfillment. And eventually I did. But it can't be a coincidence that the more time I dedicate to my career, the more fulfilling I find motherhood. Having looked at it from both sides, I can say that in my experience staying home with young children full-time was less fulfilling than working a bunch of thankless jobs. Neither fulfilled me, really, but the former debilitated me. I was losing my mind, and if I had not branched out and found something to work on, I would probably be divorced and institutionalized by now.

I have many friends who consider themselves SAHMs. But the reality is, most of them have hobbies or a side gig selling jewelry or body creams online. Even the littlest job or hobby gives them an identity other than simply Mommy. And that's really, really important.

Look, to each her own. I'm no expert, and it's certainly possible that there are mothers out there whose children totally and completely fulfill them. I just don't know any.

### ★ Five Hours in the Life ★
### of a Stay-at-Home Mom...

**5:12**      Baby wakes up and needs to eat. Feed baby. Baby won't go back to sleep in his crib and it's too early to start the day.

**5:17**      Bring baby into bed, where toddler is already sleeping because she wet the bed two hours earlier and came to spread it to ours. Lie between them, with baby on right, toddler on left, and two arms that are tingling but can't be moved for fear of waking the children. All while listening to the melodic sound of husband snoring.

**5:24**      Get kicked in the face by toddler.

**5:31**      Get kicked in the thigh by toddler.

**5:32**      Get snapped at by husband for having an unintentional family bed.

**5:39–5:42**  Tear self out of bed to change diaper that has become intoxicating. Discover that there are only three diapers left. Find Sharpie and write note on hand to buy more diapers. Accidentally rip tab of diaper off. Throw away. Circle note to buy diapers. Put baby in bouncy seat.

**5:44**       Change toddler diaper. Note to self that potty training begins TOMORROW.

**5:45–5:59**  Feed toddler breakfast. Toddler decides oatmeal makes a better art project than meal. Clean oatmeal off kitchen cabinets, ceiling, and television.

**6:00–6:31**  Feed baby the remainder of bottle. Burp baby. Catch spit with bare hands. Impress self with stellar reflexes.

**6:32**       Shove a breakfast bar down throat. Chug a cup of coffee.

**6:33–7:05**  Ignore baby to pay attention to toddler. Read to toddler. Do puzzle with toddler. Sing to toddler. "The Itsy Bitsy Spider." "You Are My Sunshine." "Puff the Magic Dragon."

**7:06–7:11**  Get baby dressed. Get toddler dressed. Use final diaper on baby.

**7:12**       Wash hands. Change shirt. Brush teeth.

**7:13–7:25**  Straighten up house, put laundry in washing machine, check email.

**7:26–7:55**  Ignore baby to pay attention to toddler. Read to toddler. Do puzzle with toddler. Sing to toddler. "The Itsy Bitsy Spider." "You Are My Sunshine." "Puff the Magic Dragon."

**7:56–8:00**   Baby leaked through clothes. Retrieve emergency diaper from car. Change clothes.

**8:00–8:12**   Load up car to head to grocery store for diapers. Buckle toddler in car seat. Buckle baby in infant carrier. Drive .05 miles only to realize diaper bag is in the garage. Turn around. Retrieve diaper bag. Proceed to grocery store.

**8:19**   Enter grocery store. Find bananas, coffee, and Advil.

**8:30**   Glance at rubbed-off Sharpie writing on hand. Attempt to decipher. Think, it can't be important.

**8:33**   Depart grocery store. Load children into car. Realize story time about to begin at bookstore. Drive to bookstore for story time. Story time started at 8:30. Interrupt story time. Sit down and listen to story.

**8:40**   Smell a dirty diaper. Remember what that note was and that there are zero diapers in diaper bag. Glance at other mothers. Zero in on mother of baby and beg for diaper. Success! Change diaper on floor. Ignore dirty looks.

**9:15**   Leave bookstore and return to grocery store. Purchase diapers. Toddler needs to go potty. Bring toddler to restroom. Watch with horror as toddler dips hands into toilet. Scrub toddler hands. Return to line for Purell.

**9:34**      Load children back into car. Keep baby from falling asleep as if life depended on it. Open car windows. Sing "Wheels on the Bus." "The Itsy Bitsy Spider." "You Are My Sunshine." "Puff the Magic Dragon."

**9:38**      Baby giggles.

**9:40**      Baby sneezes.

**9:43**      Baby cries.

**9:45**      Turn onto street.

**9:46**      Baby falls asleep.

**9:47**      Unload baby from car. Baby wakes up. So much for baby's nap.

**9:50–10:11**      Ignore fussy baby to pay attention to toddler. Read to toddler. Do puzzle with toddler. Sing to toddler. "The Itsy Bitsy Spider." You Are My Sunshine." "Puff the Magic Dragon."

**10:12**      Glance at clock. Yawn. Look at hand and wonder what note says. Question how on earth it can't even be noon.

## *Lie #20*

# IT'S JUST A PHASE

For years we've been assuming our daughter is just in an annoying phase. Turns out, she's actually just really annoying.

*—Scary Mommy Confession #254512*

Lily went through a couple-of-week span where she asked "why" so many times that I still suffer post-traumatic stress when I hear the word, more than six years later. It's just a phase, everyone told me. She'll grow out of it. And she did. Thank goodness.

There was a several-month period where two-year-old Ben refused to leave my arms for even a minute. It would have been sweet if it hadn't included trips to the bathroom and all three meals. It's just a phase, everyone told me. He'll grow out of it. And he did. Thank goodness.

Evan picked his nose so often and so intensely when he turned four that I was convinced he'd do permanent and irreparable damage to his nostrils. It's just a phase, everyone told me. He'll grow out of it. And he did. Thank goodness.

But what happens when your kids *don't* outgrow those unpleasant periods? When does a "phase" become a trait, or worse a . . . bad personality?

All you have to do to see that not all phases are outgrown is go to any mall in America on a Saturday afternoon. There's the middle-aged woman talking so loudly on her cell phone, it's as if she is single-handedly trying to cure deafness. I'm sure her parents simply thought she was going through a loud-talker phase back in the day. Then there is the man walking in front of you, meandering aimlessly from left to right and making it impossible for you to pass by him. I bet his parents thought his zigzag way of walking was cute when he was a toddler. And what about all the people in the food court chewing with their mouths open wide enough for you to get a good sense of the sogginess of the lo mein noodles? Their parents never bothered to tell their kids to chew with their mouths closed, because . . . it's just a phase!

All of the books tell us to embrace our kids' differences, to foster and celebrate their idiosyncrasies. And I believe that to a degree; there's nothing wrong with a little boy who wants to play with a Barbie doll, or a little girl who prefers the company of books to that of her classmates. *Those* are phases we should get on board with.

But when I see Lily competing to the death in every single thing she does, I force myself to resist the tendency to blame it on a phase. When your third-grade daughter is so competitive that she can't even play Pickup Sticks without hurting someone, you have no choice but to step in. Because if I don't, next thing

I know I'll be bailing her out of jail for a drunken game of Quarters gone wrong. I know her competitive streak is not a phase. It's part of her nature, and it always will be. But if I work now to help her rein it in and channel it into something productive, I think it will end up being one of the qualities that make her a successful adult.

I take the same outlook with Ben and his stubbornness. That kid will not do something if he doesn't want to. I remember when I first noticed this side of him, when he was about four. It's just a phase, I told myself, after I forbade him from eating anything until he ate one piece of broccoli—and he didn't eat anything for twelve hours, until I caved. I'm working on ways to embrace rather than antagonize stubborn Ben, because I realize it is part of who *he* is.

And Evan's tendency to RUN—rather than walk—everywhere he goes and the fact that he body-slams his family and friends as a salutation may very well be a phase. Or it could develop into one hell of an annoying personality trait. If it continues, I'll most definitely have to find some way to better channel his intense physical energy, or we'll all end up in trouble. And with some hefty ER bills to boot.

My kids are all young, and the moment I feel like I've mastered how to deal with a certain phase, they enter another, leaving me entirely clueless. I think the best I can do as a parent is help guide them to be the type of person that *I'd* want to spend time with and hope that society agrees. A motherly civic duty, and a public service to the rest of the world. Lord knows, we could use fewer annoying people around here, and I can only avoid that trip to the mall for so long.

# ★ *Phases Kids Should Never Outgrow* ★

• **THE TOO PERFECT TO LAST PHASE** when Mommy is the most beautiful person in the world.

• **THE EASY TRANSFER PHASE** when they fall asleep in the car and can be placed—still sleeping—directly into their beds.

• **THE FREE MAID PHASE** when they love dusting, vacuuming, and wiping counters for you.

• **THE PRE BAND-AID PHASE** when a kiss from Mommy cures any ailment.

• **THE EASY TO PLEASE PHASE** when the box was just as much fun to play with as the present inside.

• **THE SWEET BREATH PHASE** when even morning breath is delicious smelling.

• **THE "I'LL GET IT FOR YOU!" PHASE** when highly energetic children retrieve your every last desire.

• **THE TWO NAP A DAY PHASE** when you could actually get things done.

• **THE MOMMY IS ALWAYS RIGHT PHASE** when "because I said so" is enough of an answer for everything.

## ★ Phases They Can't Outgrow Fast Enough ★

• **THE KNOW IT ALL PHASE** when they are suddenly the smartest people in the universe.

• **THE CAN I HAVE THIS PHASE** when they expect to get whatever their heart's desire the moment they desire it.

• **THE I WANT TO PICK MY OWN OUTFITS PHASE** when they insist on leaving the house looking ridiculous.

• **THE WHY PHASE** when all you want them to do is shut the hell up.

• **THE JINX PHASE** when it's the most hilarious thing in the world when two people speak at the same time.

• **THE CONSTANT SNOT PHASE** when they have a runny nose all winter. And winter lasts from October to May.

*Lie #21*

# YOU WILL SUCCUMB TO SENTIMENTALITY

I emptied out and threw away the contents of my daughter's backpack without thinking. She's twenty and still hasn't forgiven me for ruining the self-portrait she worked on all year.

—*Scary Mommy Confession #254979*

There is little that is sweeter than a handmade macaroni necklace presented to you by your adorable toddler. The first time you receive one, you will, no doubt, proudly wear it around your neck like it was made from the finest cultured pearls. Your precious child painstakingly threaded each individual piece of pasta! With his bare hands! Look at that color composition—look at that sense of style! It's a masterpiece, and you are the luckiest mommy in the world.

Macaroni necklaces are followed by more macaroni necklaces, until you start to feel like the hostess at a Macaroni Grill.

Soon other trinkets make their way into your life, one at a time. A paper weight here. A wind-chime there. Before you know it, your house is overridden with keepsake memorabilia that threaten your sanity.

It's a tough situation to find yourself in, suddenly facing your very own Sophie's Choice: your children's feelings or your own sanity. I remember the moment I made the choice myself, swimming in piles of the kids' artwork as I tried to organize our files. It was then and there that I decided there had to be a better way. There had to be a compromise. And so began my career as a selective curator of kids' shit.

Once I decided on my course of action, I was all in. I was committed to ridding the house of excess junk that the kids made, while maintaining a respectable amount of memorabilia. There was no room for emotions, and I had to take no prisoners. And so I purged. And purged some more. I weeded out their handiwork by category: useless, dangerous, and ugly. Wouldn't you know it, about 90 percent of the stuff fit into one of the three. Frankly, there were a few times I had trouble picking just one category! I ended up with a nice smattering of keepsakes, each one bringing me back to a place and time.

That was a turning point for me as a mother. That was the moment when I put my sentimentality for children's artwork in check and reclaimed my house.

These days, it takes a lot for an item handmade and brought into this house by one of my children to last the night. I have to work quickly and quietly to avoid hurting anyone's feelings, but so far, so good. There have been paintings and tongue compressor puppets. Mugs and pillowcases and plates and clay. The list is never-ending. We haven't had any tears yet—from me or from them. And we are all better for it.

I'll never forget the time I drove to a Dumpster in the parking lot of our local Walgreen's so that I could discreetly and permanently dispose of the first semester's bounty. I waited until the kids were asleep and pulled up just as the store was closing. To my initial chagrin, I wasn't alone. There was another family-sized SUV parked near the Dumpster as I drove up. I watched as the driver stepped out of the car, opened her automatic trunk, and pulled out a kitchen trash bag. She walked over to the Dumpster, hurled the bag over her head into the trash, and got back in her car and drove away. With the coast clear, I got out of my car with my very own trash bag and made my way toward the Dumpster. As I walked to the perimeter of the big blue box, something caught my eye. It was a hole in the bag that the other women had just deposited. And there, sticking out of the hole, was something that was clearly made by a child with preschool teachers who get a good laugh at Mommy's expense.

Perhaps I was predisposed to have a weak sense of sentimentality. With a mother as sentimental as mine, I am sure that the need to rebel is partially to blame for my urge to purge. I'm also quite confident that my kids will hold on to every last thing to compensate for their mother's excessive trashing. Save too much, save too little . . . we mothers just can't win. The best we can do is choose what to save wisely. And, of course, use the utmost discretion when disposing of the rest of the crap.

# ★ Excuses to Make When Your Child Finds ★ His/Her Art in the Recycling Bin

Honey, that's not the recycling bin. I've been using it to transfer my most treasured items upstairs for storage!

Ugh! I told your dad that was IMPORTANT!

The picture you drew yesterday was soooo much better than the one you drew last week! I didn't think you wanted to keep the old one around.

I'm so sorry! I thought that was your brother's!

I'm just trying to save the planet, sweetie. You know, for *your* future.

I'm recycling it so its beauty will be with us forever! Every time I drink a can of soda or use a paper bag from now on, I'll be thinking of your beautiful art!

That's the garbage collector's Christmas gift, honey! He'll LOVE it!

*Lie #22*

# MOTHERS HAPPILY SHARE

Sometimes, I want to act just like my toddler twins. That's mine! Give it back! Not fair! Stop taking my things! And then I remember I'm the mother and nothing actually belongs to me anymore.

*—Scary Mommy Confession #257102*

There are few things in life that make me as happy as Thai food. If my husband needs to apologize for something, there's no better way to say it than with some satay. When I find myself traveling alone to a new city, the first thing I do is look up Thai restaurants on Yelp to plan my lunches and dinners. On the rare occasion when I choose where we eat as a family, rather than the children dictating, there is no doubt where I will choose. My kids groan and pick on nothing but plain white rice and the maraschino cherries that decorate the plates, but I don't care; they'll make up for it at the next meal and . . . leftovers! Thai is the only food I never tire of and always crave. Life is just too short not to enjoy good food, and to me, there is simply nothing better than Thai.

For years, I'd been the only one in my family to enjoy deliciousness like Pad Thai and Pad See Ew and Massaman Curry and Tom Kha Gai. It would be so nice to enjoy my favorite food as a family, I'd think again and again. And so I dragged them to restaurant after restaurant, trying to find one that satisfied their picky taste buds. I tried bribing them and reasoning with them and tricking them into trying new dishes, but no tactic was successful. I finally accepted that I was the sole Thai eater in the house and began ordering accordingly. One appetizer and one main course, since I was the only one eating.

Until the day last year when everything changed.

"This is yummy," Lily announced as she tentatively tasted some of my chicken satay. "Does it always taste like this?" I watched as she wolfed it down, bogarting the peanut sauce for her chicken and leaving me with the random piece of toast I never know what I'm supposed to do with. "I know it's yummy, Lily. It's the best." I smiled at her, gritting my teeth as she eyed the Pad Thai, steaming under the plastic lid. "Think I'll like that, too?"

Had I not been alone in the house with my three kids and dog, I would have grabbed the box and run for dear life. Even *with* the kids and the dog, the thought crossed my mind. "I'm not sure, Lily. There are shrimp in there. You know, from the bottom of the ocean. You might not like it." Much to my dismay, not only did she like it, but she loved it. It was one of those parenting moments where you can see your child blossoming right before your very eyes. Her horizons were broadening. She was moving out of the grilled cheese phase and into one of trying new things and not only accepting them, but enjoying them. She was growing up. But most of all? Bitch was eating *my* dinner, and I wasn't happy about it.

I should have known that day was only the beginning. Ever since Lily got her ears pierced last spring, my earrings have mysteriously migrated from my jewelry box into hers. She's outgrown her princess dress-up costumes, instead opting to trudge around in my high heels and wrap herself up in my scarves. She sneaks into my bathroom when I'm downstairs and tries on my makeup, thinking I won't notice the telltale signs of glittery lips and black powder around her eyes. What's mine is hers, she seems to think, regardless of how many times I tell her otherwise.

Sharing has always struck me as an odd concept. We tell our children to share everything—their books, their toys, their food . . . It's the nice thing to do, we tell them starting in preschool, and certainly the way to solve most issues at home or at school. The trouble is, sharing sucks—as a kid, and even more so as a grown-up.

Like all mothers, the list of things I've given up for my children is a mile long, and all I really ask for are a few basic things of my own. A comfortable place to sleep, for instance. But, noooo. Despite having their own beds to sleep in, at least two of my children will make their way into mine at some point during the night. I end up hanging off the bed, kneed in the face and sleeping in one of their plastic-mattress-pad-covered twin beds, just to escape them.

Or, water. In a world that is three-quarters water, is it too much to ask that I get one measly glass to myself? Apparently, it is. Without fail, every time I pour myself a nice glass of ice water and sit down to drink it, there appears a line of children asking for a sip. Were they not thirsty three seconds prior, when I was in the kitchen getting the ice, positioning the glass and pouring the water? Is there some otherworldly connection between their thirst level and my level of contentment? Between the backwash, the germs, and the fact that World War III will break out over who gets the biggest sip, I usually won't let them have any of my water. And I don't feel guilty about it. No, I will not share the water of which we have a never-ending supply. Why, you ask? Because it's mine.

The list of things I must share goes on: my bathroom sink where the kids spit their nasty toothpaste, despite having their own perfectly working sink; my iPhone, without which they make waiting for an appointment for any amount of time insufferable; even my socks, which I keep finding in Lily's drawers when I put away the laundry (and by "put away," I mean dump in a pile in her drawers). The fact that mothers begin sharing with their children in utero—maybe that's where Lily developed her fondness for Thai food, because I sure ate my fair share while pregnant with her—should be a warning flare for all of the sacrifices to come.

But I suppose this all comes with the territory. If motherhood were an ice-cream cone, it would always be one scoop short. And so I will take extra pleasure in reinforcing to my children the importance of sharing. I figure that if I have to suffer, they do, too. Besides, it will prepare them well for parenthood.

# ★ 10 Things to Do for Yourself ★ Before You Have Children...
## (BECAUSE YOU'LL NEVER DO THEM AGAIN)

1. Call in sick to work.

2. Savor your food.

3. Act spontaneously.

4. Spend money frivolously on yourself.

5. Pee with the door shut.

6. Have sex on the kitchen floor.

7. Own an impractical car.

8. Travel as much as you possibly can.

9. Wear a bikini.

10. Enjoy a lazy Saturday of doing absolutely nothing. Repeat on Sunday.

## Lie #23

# PARENTS HAVE ALL THE ANSWERS

Momma knows best—HA! Hardly! I have no idea what I'm doing. So long as you don't end up dead, maimed, in prison, or spending hundreds of thousands of dollars in intensive therapy, I'm going to call it a win.

—*Scary Mommy Confession* #199795

"Mommy, what happens when you die?"

"Mommy, what color are God's eyes?"

"Mommy, is the world ever going to end?"

Questions like these are what keep me feeling like a game show contestant every morning during the car ride to school. I don't know what it is about the morning car ride that makes my children so inquisitive and introspective, but that fifteen-minute ride has become far too heavy for a mother who hasn't yet downed her first cup of coffee. Whatever happened to "Mommy, why is the top of your hair a different color than the longer pieces?" Not particularly polite, but at least there's a pretty straightforward answer.

When faced with tough questions like this, I find myself stuck between the rock and a hard place of (a) making something up or (b) admitting to my children that I don't actually know everything after all. I can see the argument for each. Intellectually, I know of course that it's far better to simply say, "I don't know, honey"—teaching my children a valuable lesson while forcing them to seek out their own answers. But there is something so tempting about carrying on the myth of maternal omniscience as long as I possibly can. In the shallow toolbox of parenthood, it's one of our most powerful, yet fleeting, weapons.

The minute your kids realize that you, in fact, do not know everything is the minute when your household equilibrium shifts forever. Suddenly you're not all that authoritative anymore. Not that impressive. And once the seal is broken, it all comes undone. Not only do your kids stop asking you questions, but they actually start *challenging* what you say. From there, it's all downhill.

I remember when it first occurred to me that my own parents were fallible. It was at summer camp, on a rare rainy day. We spent those dreary days indoors, watching movies and playing games. In between braiding hair and licking orange cheese puff dust off our fingers, we listened to the *Free to Be You and Me* soundtrack to pass the time. There, on the floor of the community room listening to Marlo Thomas belt out "Parents Are People," my life forever changed. "Parents are people," she sang. "People with children. When parents were little they used to be small, like some of you. And then they grew."

It was an epiphany of earth-shattering proportions. My life was now divided between the time before the realization, when everything was simple and made sense, to after. The after was the beginning of the end.

Whatever it takes, I'm going to maintain the façade of knowing everything with my own children for as long as possible. I know the stakes are high, and I'm not throwing in the towel without a fight. As far as God's eyes, the answer is blue.

I'm sure of it.

## CONCLUSION

I've heard, on many occasions, that if women knew exactly what motherhood would entail, none of us would ever become mothers. That's the reason for all the lies, right? If we were honest with one another about how hard it truly is, would anyone in their right minds sign up for the job?

It's irrelevant, though, because nobody—not even me and my book of lies—can prepare you for what to expect once you have children. It's more challenging and frustrating and exhausting and demanding than you can possibly imagine. It will bring you to the brink of insanity repeatedly. Endlessly. To infinity.

But is it worth it? Is there a reason that people keep popping out babies and civilization hasn't yet come to a screeching halt? Do the positives *really* outweigh the negatives? That's the real question, isn't it? And the answer is an unequivocal yes. Yes, you bet your ass they do.

At the end of the day, that's the only truth you really need to know.

# ★ Parental Lessons ★

## LEARNED THE HARD WAY

**1.** Superglue has no place in a house with young children.

**2.** Neither do Sharpies.

**3.** There is no such thing as allowing your kid to play with your phone "just once."

**4.** Never use Google to diagnose illnesses. Ever.

**5.** Dollar-store toys cost far more than a dollar, in frustration, anguish, and regret.

**6.** Look in the oven before you turn it on.

**7.** Always carry wipes, long after diaper wearing has ended.

**8.** Resist stocking the house with character Band-Aids, unless you're prepared to buy a box a week.

**9.** Always keep emergency snacks hidden in the car.

**10.** Bunk beds are far more trouble than they're worth.

**11.** Keep track of who gave what at birthday parties.

**12.** Never stock D batteries in your house, or you will be forced to make obnoxiously loud toys work after they've thankfully died.

**13.** Buy Mr. Clean Magic Erasers in bulk.

**14.** Back up your photos.

**15.** Better yet, print them.

**16.** There is no point in making beds.

**17.** Accept the fact that you will inevitably turn into your mother.

**18.** Always check pockets before washing clothes.

**19.** There is no such thing as "running" into Target with children.

**20.** Take more video.

**21.** Skipping a bath one night (or two) won't kill them.

**22.** Find young babysitters and groom them. The less attractive, the better.

**23.** Always have ample one-dollar bills on hand for lost teeth and bribery.

**24.** Practice caution when approaching that stray raisin on the floor. It's probably *not* a raisin.

**25.** Keep expensive cosmetics out of arm's reach.

**26.** The four-year-old checkup is brutal.

**27.** Always look before you sit down to pee.

**28.** Train your children to clean up all LEGOs before bed, since nothing is more painful than stepping on a LEGO with a bare foot at midnight.

**29**. Save "no" for when it really matters.

**30**. Overapply sunscreen.

**31**. Don't take their word for it when children say they don't need to pee before leaving the house.

**32**. Never pay full price for kids' clothes. They always go on sale and the expensive ones inevitably get ruined first.

**33**. There's a reason why people surprise their kids with trips to Disney: *their* anticipation may kill you.

**34**. No child went to college with a pacifier.

**35**. Lock your bedroom door.

**36**. And your bathroom one.

**37**. Never open a can of soda handed to you by a child.

**38**. Walk away from temper tantrums.

**39**. Or record them for future enjoyment.

**40**. Upset as you may be, hair grows back.

**41**. But not on Barbie dolls, so hide the scissors.

**42**. Never buy more than two pairs of shoes at once. Their feet will inevitably grow once you do.

**43**. Give away the books you can't stand reading.

**44**. TV won't *really* turn their brains to mush.

**45.** Don't buy any toy that is meant to come apart, unless they can put it back together themselves.

**46.** Keep a well-hidden stock of lollipops.

**47.** Don't allow Play-Doh on carpets.

**48.** Or in the house at all.

**49.** A bathroom in a house with boys will *never* smell clean.

**50.** The moment you think you have mastered motherhood, your children will prove you wrong.

## SCARY MOMMY CONFESSIONS

My husband is higher maintenance than my children. He is more emotionally draining, demanding, and prone to temper tantrums than my preschooler.

I had every intention of buying a movie for the family tonight. Instead, I bought myself Fifty Shades of Grey.

I've been a mom for six years and still don't turn my head when I hear the word mommy. Even when it's my kid who's said it.

My children think that the Disney Store at the mall is DISNEY WORLD. They tell their friends they have been to Disney a hundred times.

I arranged a bulk pickup for a broken table as the kids screamed and bickered in the background. As I hung up, the rep asked if I wanted them picked up as well. I actually considered it.

Our baby monitor picks up the signal from our neighbors' monitor. I find myself sitting with my ear pressed against the receiver so I can listen in on them more than I'd like to admit. Being a SAHM has made me so bored and nosey.

I walk into the kitchen, open all the cabinets, and have no idea why I'm there.

With tears glistening in my eyes, I make sure to say those three wonderful words to my precious child every single day: "It's bedtime, son."

Julia Roberts says her kids wake "smelling of promise." My kids wake smelling of urine.

I feel like I got sold a bill of goods with all the talk about how much fun parenting is. Um, compared to what, a root canal?

My five-year-old daughter just took a shit in the middle of the backyard. I don't know if I should laugh or cry.

I lie to my kids daily. The park is closed; we can't go. Ice cream costs two hundred dollars; we can't afford any. Puppies eat little girls; we can't have one. Grandma has a boogeyman in her closet; tell Daddy you don't want to go.

I keep waiting for motherhood to click with me. My kids are seven and nine.

I have turned into one of the women I used to pity. The ragged, flustered, frustrated mother who struggles to control her rambunctious children while attempting to run errands.

I told my son we don't allow sleepovers at other people's houses, but the truth is, I just can't stand his best friend.

Today I left work twenty-five minutes early. I didn't go straight home. I went to a bar, where I sat and drank a beer and played with my phone. No one talked to me. It was lovely.

I fear that in contrast to overinvolved, hyperanxious helicopter moms, I am a submarine mom. Half the time I'm like, "Has anyone seen my son?"

I tell my kids everything will "make them die." It's easier. Go in the street, you're dead. Fall out of a tree, you're dead. Ask Mommy to get up and put cartoons on at 6 a.m. on Saturday, you're dead.

Sometimes my kids' voices are like nails on a chalkboard. I miss the days before they could talk.

I make mean faces at my friend's annoying two-year-old when she's not looking. She just thinks he's going through a crying-for-no-reason phase.

No idea why, but my son is PETRIFIED of a carrot nose that came in a snowman kit. It's terrible, but sometimes I take it down from the closet and say "Oh, what's this?" just to scare him. He runs screaming. I die laughing.

The intention was to sneeze gracefully with my face covered. The execution? Right as I sneezed I had to grab my crotch to keep from peeing myself. These are not the mom decisions I envisioned.

I wish parenting came with an instruction manual. That's why I sometimes would rather be at work, because I already know what's expected of me.

My daughter skipped class and instead of confronting her about it I posted on her Facebook page, "Where were you during third period today? Inquiring minds would like to know, young lady!" Hopefully the teasing from her classmates will keep her from doing THAT again.

My eight-month-old is like a dog. When you ask if she wants a bath she runs to the closet for the towel and washcloths, then runs to the tub. Good girl, now sit.

My son said to me recently, "Mommy, move your big butt. I can't see the TV." Our TV is sixty inches wide.

I bought a bottle of vodka last week at the store. This week I bought three. The clerk remembered me. I shrugged and said, "One for each kid."

Nothing like a family vacation to make you regret the decision to have children. All the stresses of home, plus all the delightful stresses of unfamiliar places and routines.

My kids frequently ask to play with my stomach flap. For FUN.

I turn the music up so I can't hear the kids. I'm pretty sure that if one of them gets hurt the other one will come tell me about it.

In response to my daughter's recent aversion to nudity, I've started wandering around the house in various states of undress. I'm hoping it'll nudge her toward a healthy body image but so far it's just nudging her to say things like "Please put some clothes on, Mom!"

The real prep for motherhood was the dump I took on the delivery table with my first daughter. Haven't gone to the bathroom without an audience since.

My four-year-old and I went to the store and as we're going past the wine rack he points and says loudly, "Mommy do you need more juice?"

Sometimes when my husband snores so loudly that I can't sleep, I imagine pushing him off the edge of the bed. I don't do it, though, because the noise of his fat ass hitting the floor would probably wake up the kids.

I accidentally caught a glimpse of my naked self in the mirror today and was horrified. I literally didn't recognize my body.

My friends all felt guilty returning to work after maternity leave. I, on the other hand, couldn't wait and didn't feel a bit of guilt.

Would it be wrong to send the teacher a bottle of vodka on the first day of school? With my kid, she's going to need it.

I just dusted my daughter's Barbie Townhouse. Where did I go wrong in life to end up as Barbie's maid???

My husband and I love to kiss extra long just to gross our teens out. I figure it's the best birth control we can offer them.

My daughter likes to dress up as me in my heels and briefcase. Little does she know, I still feel like I'm dressing up as my own mother every single day.

I have a fake front tooth. For fun, I take it out to scare young children.

I haven't talked to a single adult in three and a half days. I'm not sure I even remember how.

When my kids ask me to stop singing I just get louder. I remember hating when my mom did that to me and I'm more than happy to carry on the tradition.

My dad used to stick straws up his nose and pretend to be a walrus in restaurants to embarrass me. I can't wait to do the same.

My daughter volunteered to be the first kindergartner to share about her family in front of the class and parents on the first day! So proud! That is, until she said, "My mommy has the most prettiest and shiniest earrings in her boobies!"

Is it wrong of me to admit that I'm looking forward to embarrassing the hell out of my kids? I think of it as some sort of payback for their terrible toddler antics.

My kid's awkward phase is embarrassing ME.

Last week, I saw a new doctor. The paperwork asked if I was sexually active, so I said yes. "What do you do?" the doctor later asked in the exam room. I told her I normally did vaginal, but sometimes anal. She meant for work.

There's nothing like calling my five-foot, eight-inch teenage son "Punkin" in front of his friends.

The only reason I don't divorce my compulsive-liar husband is because I love being a stay-at-home mom. If there was some way to make a living off finger painting and gardening with my kids, I'd be gone in a heartbeat.

My kids complained about my cooking for the fifth night in a row. Instead of responding like an adult I threw the pan in the sink, screamed, "You never like anything I make!" and stomped out of the room. I'd say that went over well.

I never need to ask, "Do I look fat in this?" Everyone in my house will happily inform me if I do, without my even asking.

I bought myself an iPhone six months ago. I wonder if my son will ever let me use it.

Motherhood: a state of being that includes acting as a police chief, parole officer, maid, chef, chauffeur, laundry service, nurse, nutritionist, and therapist, simultaneously.

I consider it a victory every day my children don't kill each other.

Just asked a new friend how her kids were. She said "perfect in every way." Uh-huh, right. Sorry we can't be friends. I don't associate with liars.

I'm writing a sequel to Go the Fuck to Sleep. It is called Leave Me the Fuck Alone and Play with Your Toys.

A stranger just asked me if I was carrying twins. I'm not. But he may be walking funny for the rest of the week.

I made a Onesie for my daughter that said "If my mommy wanted your opinion, she would have asked." She only wears it when we visit my mother-in-law.

Whenever my husband acts like an ass, I change his ringtone back to "I'm sexy and I know it." He has no idea how to change it himself and has to wait for me to do it for him. Insert evil laugh.

I have started to use my naked body as a weapon so I can have some privacy. I announce that I will be naked in my room, actually BUCK naked, and they stay FAR away.

I used to live for weekends. Now, as a stay-at-home mom, I live for them to be over. Get out of my house, people!

My mental checklist when leaving the house actually has "pants" on it. Pants? Check.

I can push out a child the size of a bowling ball, lactate, go to the bathroom with an audience, and have a cold without whining that the world is ending. No one with a penis seems capable of any of these things.

My son's teacher called to tell me he had failed to turn in a major art project they'd been working on at school. I told her I'd talk to him about it, but the truth was I threw it out. I thought it was trash!

I fantasize A LOT about being single with no kids.

Before babies and breastfeeding my breasts were like giant grapefruits, all perky. After two babies and breastfeeding they now resemble deflated bananas that hang so low they nearly touch my navel.

My daughter just handed me back my phone and asked why there were dirty words on it. Um, because I was sexting your father, honey. Can you please unlearn how to read now?

I stay up to 3 a.m. every night just so I can get some quiet time away from my husband and son. Husband thinks I have insomnia. Nope, I have "leave me the fuck alone-ia."

After three kids, all by C-section, I'm not as taut as I wish I was. My son is kind enough to point out that others notice, too. One time he pointed at my mom pouch and asked, "Why does your stomach look like a bag of apples?" A bag of apples? Fuck you, kid.

I give my kids candy all day because it's easier to say yes than listen to them cry all day. They still cry all day.

Spent ten minutes trying to figure out why my Crock-Pot wouldn't turn on, only to realize I never plugged it in.

I regret all the sex I could've had before this married post-baby body turned to mush. I was hot and I didn't even know it.

Today, I was sitting at my desk and thought, Oh, I need to take my medicine. Turned, opened the desk drawer, stared at my purse, and went, "What did I open this for?"

I overheard my child's teacher telling another mom her son was a "favorite." She had told me the same thing on MY conference day. Maybe she only says this to the incredibly gifted children?

After a long hard day and getting some me-time finally, I sat down to watch TV . . . tried to use my phone as the remote . . . thought the battery was dead and kept hitting it.

I lose my car pretty regularly . . . no, not the keys . . . the actual whole big SUV. I can never remember where we parked because I was chasing a toddler or something.

I should probably care that the baby is currently chewing on one of the cat's toys.

Either my son learns to start using words INSTEAD of grunting and pointing, or his voice box is a goner.

Every night I go to sleep I tell myself I'm going to be a better mom in the morning. Five minutes after waking up I have already failed.

I have always felt like I am a horrible stay-at-home mom. Turns out, I am really good at it. As long as the kids are in school.

I didn't notice I had two different shoes on until the end of the day, when one of my kids pointed it out to me.

I was told that my boobs would go back to normal when I was done breastfeeding. Umm, normal isn't down by my knees with stretch marks.

Tonight I had a moment where I realized I'm officially a mom: I mixed vodka with a Capri Sun because we're out of OJ.

I knew that my children would suck the milk out of my breasts. What I didn't realize was that they would suck the life out, too.

I was so proud when my daughter ran off to kindergarten without even a backward wave. And then I realized she ran off without even a backward wave.

My mother-in-law told me, "It gets easier once they can walk and talk and go to the bathroom themselves." Um, yeah, right now at seven I can't put her in a crib and walk away if I need to; instead she follows me around everywhere. Easy?

I can't help but enjoy my baby more than my other two kids. He can't talk back, doesn't demand a thing, and is happy just to be held.

The real reason I've been making a huge deal about getting a family portrait done this year is that I've just lost a bunch of weight and I want to record it. AND I want to flaunt my new skinny jeans.

You know what's sweeter than the sound of a child's laugh? The sound of no freaking kids.

I'm so brainwashed by my kids' TV choices that I find myself still watching iCarly long after they've left for school.

My son started walking this week and first on his list of accomplishments was pulling a two-liter bottle of Coke off the kitchen counter. Why did we encourage this new trick?

I came home to a beautifully clean house, dishes done, laundry folded and put away, dinner cooked, baby in PJs and bathed. My husband was there with a dozen roses and a bottle of wine . . . then I woke up.

I spent most of yesterday's car ride fantasizing about pulling the car over, kicking my two fighting kids out, and peeling the hell out of there while blasting some music and flipping them off.

People wonder why many stay-at-home moms drink. How would you deal with tiny monsters terrorizing your every waking moment?

I don't understand parents who brag about how gifted and smart their kids are. Congratulations! You gave birth to a giant nerd.

Found myself arguing with my nine-year-old about her "unfair" bedtime and she won. I just extended it by thirty minutes for her. How did this happen?

I need a mom jar. Anytime the kids say MOM they put a dollar in the jar. I would have enough for a cruise in no time.

I ached for the day when my kids wouldn't pepper me with questions ALL DAY long. Now they second-guess my answers instead. I preferred the old way.

Before children, I was meticulous about how my laundry was done. Nowadays, I have two piles: a pile with shit on the clothes and a pile with ACTUAL SHIT on the clothes. This is my life.

When my son throws irrational temper tantrums, I have the urge to stick him in an ice-cold shower just to teach him a lesson.

I'm WAY nicer and more polite to my kids in public than I am in the privacy of our home.

I taught my daughter to say Dadda before Mamma so I could make my husband do whatever she needed. I pretend to be offended, but I love not having to get up in the middle of the night.

Panicked in a parking lot as I stared at the empty backseat of my car. Somebody stole my son's car seat!! Who does that!??? Oh wait . . . that wasn't my car.

Supposedly time flies when you have a kid. Yup. It sure does fly—my clock flew against the wall during my two-year-old's tantrum. Then it moved pretty damn slow.

We thought it was SOOOO smart to get Your Baby Can Read. Nope . . . she's three, and she knows what we're talking about if we say T-O-Y or P-A-R-K. So much for spelling it to keep her from knowing things.

I had to write a note on my Google calendar as to when my last shower was because I have not been finding/making time to take one regularly.

My babysitter caught my son with his pants around his ankles, swinging his diaper above his head and dancing in her living room. I am wondering if I should mentally prepare myself for him to grow up to be a stripper.

If mothering was a paid position, I would be SO fired.

I think that having kids is like living in a frat house . . . it's always loud, someone's always crying, and there's always throw-up where you least expect it.

Master chefs my ass . . . I'll call them masters when they can do all that cooking with a toddler glued to their leg and two teens already complaining that they're not going to like it before they even know what's for dinner.

You know you might have punched it a little too hard getting on the freeway when: your three-year-old raises both arms and says "Wheeeee!"

I keep a spoon in the glove box for eating Ben & Jerry's in the grocery store parking lot.

I made my two-year-old make a sad face while I took a picture and then sent it to my mom and said the face was made because she missed her grandma. Really I just needed a break and wanted my mom to babysit.

Today I'm dressed as a grumpy bitch who needs more coffee. Same costume I wore yesterday.

I found my son sitting at the kitchen table counting (unused) tampons. I left him to it. He was counting them correctly and he was being quiet and entertained without my help. Can't beat that!

I bitch and moan about having to play Santa for Christmas, but secretly I'm glad I get to fill stockings because I'm all out of Halloween candy to use as bribery or just generally steal from the kids.

I will SHED BLOOD if someone so much as flushes the toilet or turns on a light at naptime. This is serious shit, people. Naptime is sacred.

Tonight I walked in on my daughter in my bedroom singing "Summer Nights" at the top of her lungs. The only problem? She was using my vibrator as a microphone.

Took a bubble bath, shaved my stuff, and put on a teeny-tiny nightie for my hubby. He was so turned on that he pulled me close for a passionate kiss. As he ran his ringers through my hair, two small LEGOs fell out.

Today I walked in on my two-year-old drawing on his floor. With poop. And a kazoo.

I do my best to treat my children equally. For example, if I steal a candy from one treat bag, I am sure to steal one from the other two as well.

Was invited to a baby shower and checked out the registry. All this expensive organic baby bedding and stuff from Restoration Hardware. Don't they realize it all just gets covered in shit and barfed on??

Last night at church, my three-year-old stood up and at the top of his lungs yelled, "We paid! Can we go now?"

I can't get rid of this damn kangaroo pouch on my stomach. Screw it. I'm just going to make it a flesh-pocket and start hiding things in there . . . like money, or weed, or little naked men that I can make dance on command.

Two weeks ago I drank too much and ended up emailing my kid's teacher a picture via Facebook. I'm pretending it didn't happen but he keeps staring at my chest at pickup time.

Every night, after supper, I hide in the bathtub and eat a Little Debbie snack.

Last week, I was caught eating Nutella from the jar. Not wanting to share, I told my kids it was poop. They, in turn, told every single one of their friends that I eat poop from a jar. Whatever. I'd do it again.

Behind all the messy rooms, horrible folding of laundry, lack of cooking skills, inability to control my toddler's tantrums, total lack of interest in crafts, and wine-drinking coping, lies the best mom ever. Really. I swear.

## ACKNOWLEDGMENTS

This book would not exist without the help and guidance of the following people . . .

My husband, Jeff Smokler. None of this would be possible without you.

My mom, Kathy Epstein. There is simply no better mother.

And the rest of my wonderful family, both immediate and extended. Thank you for your unwavering enthusiasm and excitement. I love you all.

The incredible team at Simon & Schuster, most of all: Lauren McKenna, for taking a chance and having faith in me; Karen Kosztolnyik, for being the most encouraging and awesome editor I could have asked for; and Jennifer Robinson, for putting up with me so beautifully.

Lisa Leshne, the best literary agent in the world.

My Scary Mommy Community Managers, who keep the message boards and Confessional alive and thriving: Samantha

Angoletta, Charisse Oates, Cris Salas, Love Barnett, and Mikki Caplan-Zaple. And Lily Read, for her always wise virtual ears.

Finally, the Scary Mommy community, for sharing your stories, your children, and your lives with me. Scary Mommy became the amazing and inspiring place it now is because of *you*. You have my eternal gratitude.